AGAINST THE WIND

How I Survived My Life With Grandma

by
Jenny Sturgill

Jenny Sturgill

AGAINST THE WIND
By Jenny Sturgill

ISBN: 978-1-60416-740-5

Copyright © 2015 Jenny Sturgill.
All rights reserved.

No part of the material protected by this copyright notice may be reproduced or used in any form or by any means, electronic or mechanical, including photocopying, recording, or by any information storage and retrieval system, without the prior written permission of the copyright owner.

First Printing October 2015

Williams Printing Co.
242 University Drive
Prestonsburg, Kentucky 41653
1-800-765-2464
rpublisher@aol.com

Printed in the United States of America

For my family

Jenny Sturgill

Table of Contents

Acknowledgement 7
Introduction 9
Angel in my Pocket 12
Monsters 17
My Mother 28
Bitty and Booze 37
Words to Live By 50
The Bridge 55
Becoming a Woman 64
Rising Water 73
The Janitor 83
Usher 91
Love Letters 102
Pants 112
The Hammer 119
The Witch 133
The Suit 144
Getting Married 154
Epilogue 174

Jenny Sturgill

Acknowledgement

My deepest gratitude to Mary Rosenblum for her genuine encouragement, patience, and guidance, and whose expert knowledge she most generously shared.

Thanks to my husband, Willie, for being such an insightful first editor and for always being so encouraging and supportive.

Jenny Sturgill

Introduction

I awoke early that morning, got out of bed, and looked through the window. It was still dark outside. I stood there with the curtains parted and thought about the submission I'd sent to *Page&Spine Magazine*. I'd been looking for a response every few hours since I'd sent it in a few days ago. I knew sometimes it took a long time for a response but I couldn't help checking my email. I so hoped they would accept my story. The editor had said she would be interested in a piece about retiring to writing and they actually paid money for the submissions that were published. It wasn't the money. It was the idea of having my story published in a real magazine. I had just finished a writing course and this was my first submission. I'd been warned that rejections were usual and to get used to it, because most submissions were rejected. It was a story about my retirement from a long career in nursing, and how I'd gone on to pursue writing in my retirement years. I'd missed my nursing career a lot until I started this new venture of writing, and I had put my heart and soul into that story.

Soon it was daylight and time go downstairs to

Jenny Sturgill

get my morning coffee. I took my favorite cup from the cabinet and poured myself a fresh cup of coffee. Sinking down into my easy chair by the window in the sun room I opened my email, which was crowded with the usual advertisements and junk mail. Then I scrolled down and found one from the editor of *Page&Spine Magazine*. My heart almost stopped. This was it, the rejection. I stared at the screen for a long, anxious moment. Then I took a deep breath, squeezed my eyes shut, and clicked it open. With my heart pounding in my temples I opened my eyes and read: *"We'd like to accept your story for publication."* My eyes widened and I let out a yelp of joy, jumped up, and ran to tell my husband, Willie. "I'm being published!"

I threw my arms around his waist and almost knocked him down. Quickly I phoned everyone I knew with the good news. I grinned from ear to ear as I relayed the message to my family and friends, who bombarded me with good wishes and excitement. Then I thought of Grandma. If she had still been alive, how would she have reacted? Would she finally have been proud me? I thought of her negative attitude and could only shake my head. I'd doubt if she would have reacted with any kind of joy. She was a bitter woman who had never seemed to find joy in anything. I remember growing up in all those rundown rental houses and when I look around and see all the nice comfortable things that surround me I often shudder at how my life could have turned out.

My story is about my struggle to grow up, living with my eccentric grandmother. I don't tell this to discredit her, but to show that we *can* overcome the hardships and dysfunctions that swirl around us as we grow up, that we can emerge with enough wisdom to understand how relationships work and give of ourselves to others. This book is meant to be an encouraging journey through some difficult times. It's a story of survival, resilience, and triumph.

Jenny Sturgill

Angel in my Pocket

I was lost.

That is my very first memory -- of standing in a cornfield on a river bank close to a swollen, raging river. Tears are running down my cheeks and dripping off my chin and I'm shivering in the cold rain that peppers my face and bare arms.

I didn't know where that memory came from. I must have been very young, maybe two or three.

One day, my favorite Aunt Jo called me to her and said, "Jenny, come sit with me for awhile, and let me tell you a story." I sat down beside her on the brown worn sofa. I'd just recovered from a serious illness, diagnosed as pneumonia by the old women in the community. I had had a high fever. I had been weak, and unable to raise my head off my pillow, and I drifted in and out of consciousness. With no money for medical care, we relied on home remedies for treatment. The neighbors came each night to pray and keep vigil until daylight.

And I had gotten better.

I had barely escaped death.

"Jenny, this isn't the first time. I believe you have an angel in your pocket," Aunt Jo said, as she settled in with her arm around me to tell me the story.

She told me that my cousin Edward, who was five years older than me, and our grandma and I had lived on a riverbank when I was about two years old, in a rundown rickety shack of a house that slumped from age and had posts like stilts that supported the backside. Tall corn stalks grew along the riverbank, and a two lane blacktop road ran in front of the house. Above the road loomed a steep mountain covered with trees, boulders, bare patches of soil, and long wide gullies carved by the rain. It was prone to mudslides.

The thunder rolled, lightning danced along the mountaintops, and the clouds burst, pelting rain against the windows and rooftop day and night for days. The water rushed down the hillside, creating new trenches, and pouring water into the ditch beside the road, until it swelled over onto the road, washing away pieces of blacktop on its way to the swollen river. Carrying mud along with it, it turned the river a coffee colored brown.

It was early in the day, washday for Grandma, who was boiling our clothes on the stove. Grandma was a stern woman, quick to anger, stoop-shouldered from the burden of losing her husband to a mine accident, raising five children of her own until adulthood, then having two more dropped in her lap to raise after they had left. She wore a mask of bitterness and rarely had anything good to say about anyone or anything. Edward, my seven-year-old cousin, stood looking out the back window watching logs, small sheds, and debris roll down the swollen murky river.

The mudslide came quickly and brutally, buckling our house as if it were made of matchsticks, crumbling walls, dumping mud, trees and rocks onto the top and front of the house, so that it slipped dangerously close to the swollen river.

Neighbors came from up and down the road, carrying shovels, pushing wheelbarrows, and offering their muscles to help. Grandma knew everyone from near to far, having lived in that same area for years. Strangers were unheard of in that little rural community. There was no reason for strangers to stop by; there was nothing to stop for. That's just how it was; everyone knew everyone else and their business.

Grandma and Edward weren't scalded by the pot of boiling water as everything tilted and fell, but I was nowhere to be found. I'd been asleep in my crib toward the front of the house when the mudslide hit.

Men and women shoveled dirt into wheelbarrows and hauled it away, their clothes stuck to their backs with sweat and the drizzling rain. They dragged trees, debris, and pieces of the walls and roof from the part of the house where I slept. They found nothing, not even a splinter of the crib-- nothing. Panic and fear settled over the community. The impact had surely thrown the crib with me in it in into the swift river, sweeping us away.

The search continued into the dusk, everyone now tired and beginning to lose hope. Finally, they gathered their tools and one by one, faces solemn, they plodded back to their homes. Grandma sat on a turned up bucket, the hem of her house dress trailing in the mud beside her, her head in her hands, and stared out at the raging river rushing by, muttering something no one could understand.

Edward saw him first, and called to Grandma, "Come quick." A man dressed in overalls and no shirt was walking up through the cornfield, mud sucking at his boots with every step. He was carrying something. Edward couldn't quite make it out at first; then he realized it was a small child. Could it be? It was! The man handed me, wrapped in a muddy white shirt, into Edward's arms, as if he knew where I belonged. The few neighbors still standing around muttered, "Thank God," and stared at this stranger with disbelief.

"I found her down there in the cornfield," he said, and smiled with a twinkle in his soft brown eyes. Everyone gathered around, hugging, laughing, and shouting praise. When the firestorm of commotion was over they looked around, but the man was gone.

With puzzled looks, everyone started asking questions. Who was this mysterious man, and what would a stranger be doing walking in a cornfield so near a raging river at dusk, and in such bad weather?

No one was ever able to answer those questions.

We went to Grandma's brother's house and stayed there until we could find another house to rent. Then we moved back to Boldman and took a small house behind Ralph Hamilton's store. We lived there until I started school.

Against the Wind

Monsters

I was four years old. Edward, and I were playing Sky King on the concrete floor in the back room while Grandma was somewhere else in the house doing something. "You know there're other things that live in this house besides us." He stretched his eyes wide and raised his brows. "They're liable to come through that door at any minute." He had a smug look about him as he shifted his eyes to mine. Then he pushed his plane into my cardboard ramp and turned it over. He fell and rolled, his knees drawn up, and landed on his back, sat up and looked me square in the face. "There is, I heard 'em the other night after you went to bed. I even saw 'em. They walked right past my bed, went'n stood by the couch and looked down at you." I clasped my hands together so tightly that my knuckles hurt, and looked at him wide-eyed. "They come out when they think nobody's looking." He had a mischievous look on his face and was grinning from ear to ear.

"Stop it, there is not!" I sat back on my heels and looked around at the back door, then to the door that led to the living room. Had I felt a chill or was it my imagination? Did other things really live here? You never could tell with Edward -- he was always making up some kind of tale. Deep down I believed him, and the fear began to swell up in my body. I sat still as he talked.

"Yep, they're here all right. I've seen 'em. They have horns and long sharp teeth and they are way tall, with long arms and razors for claws. They may come out any minute." He pressed his face to mine and I could feel his breath as he looked me in the eye.

"Stop it!" My vision blurred with tears. I gave him a hard shove, knocking him back on his hands. He laughed, and I held my breath as my heart banged away in my chest. All I could think about was this gang of monsters that were hiding out of sight. I felt like giving him a big kick, but I didn't because he'd just tell Grandma, and then I'd get a lickin' for hurting her precious baby boy. He was her favorite. Anyone could see that, and she'd even told us that, one time when she was drunk. I didn't like it when he teased me about scary things, but when he went to school it was like something had died inside of me. When he came home he'd bring home his books, we'd sit on the couch, and he'd teach me what he'd learned in school that day. I soon was able to read his books all the way through, just like he did. He taught me how to add, subtract, and divide.

I missed him terribly while he was in school. And now there were monsters... I moped around all day looking out the window and up the road, asking Grandma again and again if it was time for him to come home yet.

*

"Where are you going, Grandma?" It was the next day, Edward was at school, and I sat on the couch and watched as she slipped into her white sweater and tied a red head scarf over her hair.

"To the post office." She turned and wagged her index finger at me. "You just better not get into anything while I'm gone."

"Can I go with you?" I hopped down off the couch and stood by her side. Fear had begun to build inside me. While we lived in Boldman she went to the post office every day, a long walk up highway 23 and across the bridge to Hurricane Creek. It took her more than an hour to get there and back. I was too small to go all that way by myself, and Edward was at school.

"No, not today, you stay here and don't go out of this house. Hear me?" She opened the door and closed it tight behind her. I raced over to the couch, climbed up to the window, and watched as she went up the hill past Ralph Hamilton's store. Her dark blue dress flapped around her, and she was quickly hidden by the tall trees that lined highway 23. I turned, slid down, and sat on the couch for a while.

POP, CRACK

My heart leaped in my chest, and I sat frozen, waiting for the other things to come out. I finally couldn't stand it and went to the front door. A wild icy gale howled into the room as I opened the door and I shut it quick. Grandma had said to stay in the house, but I couldn't, not with those things in here that might get me any minute. My teeth chattered in fear. I couldn't even turn around. I opened the door again, stepped outside, and pulled my sweater close around me. The wind swirled up around my legs and made me shiver. I looked over to where Charlotte lived across the dirt road that ran in the back of our house. She was my best friend, who came over and played through the fence with me. She had shaggy blond hair that hung in her eyes and Grandma always called her "Shag." She wasn't allowed inside the fence Grandma had put up, and I wasn't allowed outside it. So we squatted beside the fence to play. Every time she and her mother went to town, Charlotte would say, "I'll bring you a big doll when we go to town today." I'd be so excited and I'd wait and wait by the fence until they returned, but there never was a big doll for me.

The gate flew open, and I willed my legs to dash across the road to Charlotte's house, not even looking back to our place full of monsters with horns, sharp teeth, and claws like razors. I tiptoed across the green painted porch, and rapped lightly. Her mother opened the door. Her long curly hair was still loose and tousled; the breakfast dishes were still piled in the sink. I blinked and pushed a curl out of my eye. "Can I come in and play with Charlotte?"

"Yes, of course." She had a bubbly way about her and laughed a lot. I eased inside. The scent of biscuits and bacon filled my nose as the wind sucked it out the front door. Their house was warm and comfortable compared to ours, with its bare drafty windows and monsters behind the doors. Charlotte had her own room decorated with yellow, flowered wallpaper and sheer, wispy, white curtains tied back from the window with shiny ribbon. Charlotte had made a tent with her yellow bedspread and she was under it, playing with her dolls. I climbed up on the bed and slipped under the covers. My whole body seemed to sigh with delight as I sank into the soft mattress. We played house under that tent and had real homemade cookies and milk in Charlotte's little tea set.

It was fun, but I remembered I had to get home before Grandma did. I slid through the door just as I saw Grandma coming down the road, carrying a box. I sat on the couch with my feet dangling and my hands folded in my lap. I forgot about the other things that lived in our house, because Grandma was bringing a box and that meant that our Aunt Jo had sent us something. Joy rose up from my stomach. Jo was my favorite aunt and had a sweet way about her. When I was little I'd crawl into her lap and try to pull her red fingernails off; I wanted to be just like her. I twisted and squirmed on the couch, until the doorknob turned, and the door opened.

Grandma entered, carried the box over to the kitchen table, and set it down. She let out a deep breath, opened the cabinet drawer, took out the scissors, and sawed through the tape with the open blades. I stood over to the side, my heart swelling with anticipation as she opened the top and peered inside. The monsters had gone back to wherever they lived. She pulled out a bag of stockings first. Jo always sent her a bag of stockings that didn't have too many runs in them. Grandma wore them most of the time. She pulled them just above her knees and twisted the tops into a knot, and then she tucked the knot under the roll to keep them up. Grandma had worn them that way so long that there was a permanent dent in her leg where the roll went.

Grandma never accepted charity from anyone except her children. She shooed away the church people that came to the door at Christmas, offering to give us toys and food. I was in a constant state of shame because of how poor we were and envied Charlotte her nice mother and pretty dresses. I reached in and pulled out another small box tied up with string. The scent of vanilla filled the air. She snatched it from my hand and cut the string with the scissors. Piled in the box was a whole batch of red, green and yellow iced sugar cookies. My mouth watered. Grandma raked them out of the box and into the garbage. My heart sank as I saw the cookies crumble to the bottom of the can. I could taste the creamy sweet icing and hear the crunch of the crisp cookies.

"I wish she'd quit sending that stuff here. You're not eating that nasty stuff." It didn't surprise me. She always threw away anything that was sent to us to eat. It was astonishing how she seemed to be so afraid of germs, but wouldn't let us wash our hair or brush our teeth. Grandma always said too much hair washing made your hair fall out. Even as a small child, I knew this was not normal behavior. Sometimes when Grandma was in another room, I'd sneak into the kitchen, fish the cookies out of the garbage and eat them anyway. I'd slip two or three of them under my shirt and hide them in the back room to enjoy later. I never did get sick and Grandma never caught on.

She dug deeper into the box and pulled out a small doll for me and some little trucks for Edward. But what I looked forward to the most were the half-empty bottles of nail polish hidden deep in the bottom of the box. I rammed my hand down into the box and came up with three bottles: scarlet, cotton candy, and pink ice. Grandma hardly ever let me paint my nails in the house, saying she couldn't stand the smell.

She went to the post office every day and every day I'd go over to Charlotte's house to play. I was safe from the monsters and Charlotte's mother didn't mind. One day I forgot the time and Grandma came to the door. "Is Jenny here?" I heard her yell. My heart stopped and I felt my blood rush up my neck to my cheeks. I knew I was a dead duck. She came in, grabbed my hand, and jerked me along, back across the road. My vision was already blurred by tears.

Grandma stopped in the back yard and broke off a keen, limber switch from the tree growing there. Pain shot up my legs as she whipped the switch across one leg, then the other, over and over. I let out a squall, then a sob, and the tears rolled down my cheeks. Grandma shoved me inside. "You just better not ever go there again, or I'll beat you to death. You've got no business over there!" I lay on the couch rubbing the welts on my legs and sobbing. "I won't..." I wailed. "But Grandma, there's monsters in the house. Edward told me so, and I'm afraid here by myself." I didn't understand why I couldn't just stay and play with Charlotte while she was gone instead of staying at our house with the monsters.

"That's just nonsense, there're no monsters here," she snapped. "Now shut up or I'll give you something to cry about." I sniffed and sighed.

The next time Grandma went to the post office I didn't know what to do. The door closed behind her, and I climbed up on the couch and sat on my knees. I propped my head in my hands; my elbows dug into the back of the couch, and I watched as she disappeared from sight, up the road. Pops and cracks came from the walls in the house. My heart hammered in my throat and goose bumps rose on my arms and legs. My body began to tremble. Did the back door just move? Was something there? My throat hurt with every breath. I climbed down off the sofa and scooted a straight-backed chair over in front of the back window, as close as I could get it. With my nose pressed against the window I stared over at Charlotte's house, wishing I could go there to play. To be safe.

    I couldn't. If Grandma found out, she'd kill me this time. I reached down and winced as my hand brushed over the welts still on my legs. My shoulders tightened and I jammed my hands under my armpits. The chair began to shake and my mind swirled with fear. My throat began to get tight, and I felt tears stinging. The house popped again and I felt the hair on the nape of my neck rise. I unfolded my arms, rubbed my white knuckles with my thumb and thought that this would never end. A scream struggled to escape. I knew that I was going to be devoured any minute. The floorboards sighed under footsteps behind me and I felt a hand on my shoulder. My own scream sliced the silence and my feet hit the floor. My legs went weak as I started to run. A hand squeezed my arm and pulled me back. I stifled a gasp. "Where do you think you're going?" Grandma said, as she grabbed both my arms and shook me until my teeth rattled and my head bobbled back and forth. I struggled and finally escaped her grip, opened my mouth to speak, but my voice was stuck in my throat. "Come back here you little scaredy brat. There are no monsters here."

She was wrong. But, I couldn't run.

Jenny Sturgill

My Mother

I was five years old and small for my age. On this particular morning, I rubbed the sleep out of my eyes, scooted to the side of the couch that served as my bed, and sat up. Then I stood up, used the pail we kept behind the door as a chamber pot, and padded barefoot into the kitchen. I stopped and my eyes grew wide. There by the door was a big, green, striped watermelon. Grandma was sitting at the kitchen table sipping coffee from a chipped, rose-patterned cup. I sat down cross-legged on the floor and felt the cool linoleum through my thin gown. There was a chill in the house so I pulled it down over my knees. I reached over and brushed my fingers over the cold smoothness of the watermelon and looked over at Grandma. "Why didn't you tell me Mother was here last night? Why didn't you wake me up?" Tears stung my eyes and I could feel my face droop. I always knew when my mother came to visit. She always brought a watermelon. She always came in the night while I was asleep and I never got to see her. I loved watermelon, but I'd much rather have seen my mother instead.

"She didn't stay long." Grandma got up, carried her cup over to the counter, and slammed it down into the sink among the other dirty dishes. "She thinks all she has to do is bring a watermelon and everything is fine and dandy. She never brings anything *I* need, like some money to put clothes on your back and food in your mouth. If that's all she can do I wish she'd just stay away. She always brings that no good husband with her. She's probably afraid to let go of a dime for fear he'd beat her up, like he always does. I'd just as soon she didn't come at all. Besides she's always messing around where she's got no business."

Mother seemed to come often when I was small, maybe three or four years old. Grandma didn't like it, then, either. Mother's husband seemed to make her nervous. She had married a man who wasn't the best husband in the world. He was tall and thin, with a big head of curly, dark hair. The few times they came while I was awake I would ride around in front of our house on the running board of their car as they started to leave, until Grandma would finally jerk me off and tell me to go into the house.

Grandma turned around from the sink and looked at me. "She's no good, I tell you, no good."

She came over and stooped over me. "See those scars on your legs?" She leaned over, grabbed my leg and ran her finger over the indented scars on my knee and outer right calf. "See this?" She took my hand and forced my finger to touch the scars. See, they're round, just like the butt of a cigarette. She used you for an ashtray. She's no good I tell you! She doesn't care anything about you; if she did she'd provide more for you." I jerked my hand away and covered my ears.

"No--no! Stop saying that." Fresh tears swelled up in my eyes. Surely she wouldn't do that, burn me... "She's never been mean to me."

"So why don't she take you with her--eh?" Grandma grabbed my arms and pulled me up on my feet, her grip tight around my arms. "Now get out of here. I don't want to hear any more out of you!" I ran into the living room and crawled back up on the couch, pulled my knees up to my chin, and ran my hand over the scars on my legs. Grandma had planted a seed of doubt in my mind and I began to worry. I stared down at my scars as sadness consumed me. Could it be true? I just couldn't see Mother doing a thing like that. If she did it, surely it had been an accident. Grandma's words whirled in my head like leaves caught in an autumn storm.

Two weeks later, for some reason Grandma wouldn't explain, I went with her to visit my mother. Grandma was going to leave me there for a few days while she went to tend to some kind of business she had in a town that was a few hours away. I was surprised, since she seemed to not want me to associate with my mother. It must have been very important business for her to leave me there. At the train station I followed behind Grandma, a fold of her skirt wadded in my hand. We stepped through the train doors, and Grandma handed the ticket collector our tickets as we made our way to our seats. Voices buzzed and thick smoke filled the car. We took a seat midway down the aisle, and I felt the slick cracked vinyl of the seat through my thin pants as my feet dangled above the floor. The train gave a jerk as the whistle blew its departure, on its way to Louisville, Kentucky, where my mother lived. She had told me she lived in a modest white clapboard house, with a barn that had some horses tied up in there. I couldn't wait to see it with my own eyes. My legs shook against my seat with the vibration of the train as it chugged along. I squirmed and smiled to myself, jumping up every few minutes to look out the window at the meadows and forests whizzing by. "Are we there yet?" I kept asking Grandma, who sat solemn-faced beside me.

Despite Grandma's frown, I was excited to be going to my mother's house and getting to stay with her alone. When we arrived, I needed to use the potty chair on the back porch. I felt embarrassed because it was outside, and I could see a railroad track and some houses off in the distance. I thought people riding on the train and living in the houses could see me using the potty. I'd never done my business outside, for all to see. My heart beat fast in my chest and my cheeks flamed as Grandma pulled down my pants and pushed me down on the potty. "No one can see you, they're too far away. Now stop that whining," Grandma said, grasping my shoulder so hard that it hurt.

After we settled in, I skipped down the dirt path to the barn in the distance, stopping and squatting along the way to pick a bouquet of wild daisies to take back to Mother. The big barn, its unpainted wood siding a weatherbeaten gray, stood at the end of the path. I wanted to pet the horses, so I eased the barn door open. A brown horse poked his head out. His huge head loomed over me as he let out a snort and shook his head. I screamed, dropped my bouquet, and with trembling legs, ran back up the path toward the house where Mother stood on the back porch. She opened her arms and I fell into their safety, panting for breath. She picked me up and I laid my head on her shoulder. Her hair tickled my nose and I could smell her rose cologne. She wore a simple flowered skirt with a white blouse tucked in at the waist, and her long brown hair framed her face with soft curls. She carried me into the house and set me down on the polished wooden floor. A wonderful scent filled the air. I sniffled and rubbed my eyes as she stooped down and looked me in the face. Her smile stretched across her face and made her blue-gray eyes shine and sparkle. "Shush, they won't hurt you. I'll go with you next time. Now let's go get some supper. We have ice cream for dessert." She rose, took my hand in hers, and together we hurried back into the kitchen.

    The bowl of green and purple grapes spilling out of the clear glass bowl onto my mother's dining room table made my mouth water. As I helped her, each time I passed the table I grabbed a handful and stuffed them into my mouth. I'd never had grapes to eat before. My face stretched into a grin as I closed my eyes and savored the sweet juices as each grape burst in my mouth. I just couldn't keep from grabbing more. When they were almost all gone my mother came into the dining room. Her eyes swept the table and paused at the almost empty bowl of grapes. She placed her hands on her hips and frowned. "You can't have any more of those; keep your hands out of them." My shoulders slumped. I bowed my head, gazed down at my ragged sandals, and felt guilty. My young feelings were bruised from her harsh words, but the grapes had tasted so good that I couldn't keep my hands away.

A few months later, my mother came for a visit at our house. Grandma told me she was coming. "She probably got into a fight with that no-good husband and is leaving him. If she thinks she can just come back here to stay, she's dead wrong."

I waited anxiously by the back window for her black Plymouth to drive up the road and park next to our house. Finally I saw her car pull off the road and stop out back. My heart leaped in my chest. I ran out the back door and jumped into her arms as she got out of the car. She carried me into the house and set me down on the couch. Then she went back out to get her luggage and, of course, a big juicy watermelon. I hopped off the couch and helped her carry some bags of stuff into the house. After she had settled in for a while I asked her if she would read me a story. I went to the back room and sorted through the few books that I kept in an old cardboard box, found my favorite, and carried it to her side. It had a picture of a little girl and boy on the front cover playing in a schoolyard. Some pages were torn, and they were well worn and dog eared. I held it to my chest. "Read this one," I said and handed it to her. I nestled beside her on the broken down sofa, her arm around my shoulders, my body resting in the crook of her arm, and listened as she read. I scooted as close to her as I could possibly get. I felt warm and safe sitting there in the comfort of her arms. Her voice was sweet as a bird's song and her hair fell down around her shoulders in soft curls. She smelled fresh, like a spring day after a shower.

    I wished she could stay forever, but I often heard her and Grandma in the kitchen fighting and knew that was not a good thing. In a few days she got up one morning and said, "I have to go home now." I felt a lump form in my throat and tears gathered along my eyelashes. Mother took a seat on the sofa. I crawled up into her lap, laid my head on her chest, and heard the beat of her heart. My index finger traced the soft curve of her lips and I let my hand trail down her cheek. "Will you take me with you this time?" I looked into her eyes and it was like looking into my own. She had a gentle way about her that made me feel warm and content on the inside.

Jenny Sturgill

"I can't take you this time, but I promise the next time I come, I'll take you with me." She smiled, tucking loose strands of my brown hair back away from my face and kissing my forehead. She lifted me off her lap, stood me up on the linoleum floor, went to the bedroom, picked up her suitcase, and set it beside the door. I wanted to go with her *this* time; I was tired of living with Grandma. I wanted to be with my mother all the time. I would miss Edward a lot, but I still wanted to go with her. My throat felt tight. But I didn't cry. After all, she had promised to take me the next time she came. I watched her drive away, my nose against the glass, until the car was out of sight.
I believed her and waited for her, full of anticipation. But the days became weeks and she didn't come back. I began to wonder if she had ever been there for me in the first place.

Bitty and Booze

I was six years old.

Grandma opened the door to the back room where I spent most of my days playing alone with my pet chicken, Bitty, or the few broken toys and dogeared books we kept tucked away in a cardboard box. I looked up from the doll with the missing leg that I was playing with. Grandma was leaning up against the door and almost had a smile on her face. Most of the time her mood was pretty dark, and I always knew something was most likely wrong when she entered the back room. Life with her was like sitting on the edge of a knife. I never knew what she would come up with to quarrel about. I laid the doll down in the old broken chair seat that was her bed. Grandma stood with her hands tucked into the twin pockets of her flowered apron. "There's a puppy under the floor next door. If you want to crawl under there and get it, you can."

My heart leaped in my chest and I felt my face stretch into a big smile. I hopped up and pushed past her, ran out the door and over to the empty house next door. She followed a few steps behind. "You mean it? We can really have a puppy?" I called back over my shoulder. It wasn't like Grandma to care about anything I might like, but I wasn't asking any more questions. A puppy was a puppy.

Excitement ran through my body, as I sank to my knees and crawled under the floor. The earth was cold against my palms and my overalls were getting dirty. I clawed my way through cobwebs and hanging debris. The smell of mold and dust tickled my nose, but I kept my eyes on the puppy hunched up against the slanted back wall. It hunkered down and lowered its ears as I approached, then let out a weak cry as I grabbed it by the nape of the neck. The small, warm body felt soft next to my cheek. It was a bundle of brown fur with curious eyes and little sharp teeth that gnawed at my arm. I crawled back out holding the squirming puppy close to my chest, and carried it home.

I was thrilled to have something warm to hold close to me. It had been a long time since I'd felt something so soft and warm. Grandma was right behind me, giving orders to clean up after it, and it just better not cry and bark and keep her awake at night.

"What can we name it?" I asked Grandma as we climbed the two steps to the small back porch.

"Booze, that's what we'll name it." She had a

mischievous look in her eye. Now, that name wasn't surprising, since boozing it up was Grandma's favorite pastime and she seemed to partake of booze every chance she got. I shifted the puppy to one arm, opened the screen with the other, and entered the back room. I felt something warm run down my front and saw a puddle form on the floor. I quickly grabbed a rag lying on the chair, put the puppy down, and wiped up the piddle. Then I leaned back on my heels, and watched as it went over and licked Grandma on her bare shin. Grandma pushed it away, reached down to wipe the slobber off her leg with the hem of her grey skirt, then turned and left the room. I stood, clasped my hands close to my chest, and bent down to pick up the little ball of fur. I draped it over my shoulder the way I did with my dolls. My own little puppy!

    I was lonely, playing by myself, after Edward went off to school. We had both come to live with our grandmother when our mothers decided they could no longer care for us. We were both quite small at the time. Both of us were born out of wedlock, and that seemed to crush Grandma's pride. She never got over it. It was a disgrace in her eyes and I felt that she blamed us for it, as if we were responsible for her unhappiness. Grandma had turned into a monster about anything that might be remotely sexual. But that was something I'd discover later on. Right now, I had the puppy, and she filled the hole that Edward had left in my life when he went to school.

*

Grandma seemed to like my pet chicken, Bitty, too. We got her a few years before Booze came along.

Our neighborhood was tight, a place where we almost felt our neighbors' breath on our faces. Most folks rented their homes, but the Ferrells lived across the dirt road, and we considered them well-to-do. They even owned a car.

Mr. Ferrell came over one day, holding a broken-legged chicken in his arms. "I hit this chicken with my car. It's yours for supper," he said, handing it across the wire fence to Grandma.

Now, our grandma wasn't one to take handouts, she was even too proud to accept the commodities offered by the government; the bags of flour and pinto beans, cans of peanut butter, and great hunks of American cheese that came in plain wrappers, and were free for the asking. Sometimes neighbors would give us things, saying that they somehow ended up with too much. Deep down I felt she appreciated their kindness. Grandma accepted the chicken.

Edward and I begged her to let us have the chicken for a pet. Our grandma was stubborn, with liquid black eyes that could stare a hole clear through to your soul. She gave us a stern look. "No, we are having it for supper, enough said." Her voice was firm and steady.

Edward was much better at persuasion than me, born with the gift of gab, and older. I was the timid one. I usually stood on the sidelines and cheered him on.

"See how scared it is," Edward said.

"It won't be scared long, it'll be dead," she said, kicking through tall grass with her run-over shoes, heading for the back yard to wring its neck. We trotted behind, Edward pleading a good case for the chicken. I think he wanted it more for me than himself, knowing how much I liked animals.

Her face finally softened and she let us keep it. Joy filled our hearts, even if it was just a black, broken-legged chicken. I carried it to the back room where I played most of the day, and set the chicken down on the cold concrete floor. I ripped up strips of newspapers and fashioned a nest in a box. The chicken seemed content, as if it knew it had been saved from the frying pan.

"Let's name it Bitty," I said, and Edward

agreed.

Days went by; Bitty ate her chopped corn and drank water from a bowl inside the box. We played long hours in that little back room, just Bitty and me. Edward went to school, and for me, the chicken filled the long lonely days. Her legs healed, and she grew strong, running close by my side everywhere I went.

We played dress up together, me and that chicken. I had some old make-up from Aunt Jo sent in boxes of clothes and things she had grown tired of. Grandma didn't approve of makeup, never wore any herself, and disapproved of those who did. I don't know if she approved of chickens wearing makeup or not, she never said.

I painted Bitty's bill with the reddest lipstick ever, and painted her toenails to match, powdered her face with face power, so that her black eyes looked like black dots on a white wall. I fashioned dresses from old scraps of material and constructed little shoes with sleeves for her toes, like the fingers of a glove. She even donned a red bonnet, tied at her throat with a shiny red ribbon. Bitty didn't seem to mind. I suppose getting dressed up beat a hot skillet full of grease any day.

Biddy would come running at the sound of Grandma tapping the side of the bowl filled with crumbs that Grandma had saved for her. Grandma often went to the garden and turned up the rich black dirt with a hoe, looking for worms. At times like these Grandma almost seemed normal. She'd take the hoe from beside the house. "Let's go get worms for Bitty," she'd say with a ghost of a smile playing along her thin lips. I'd almost forget her odd ways and could snatch a few moments of happiness from the situation. She'd dig as I squatted down and sifted through the black earth, pulling out slimy worms. Bitty would scratch up the fresh dirt, turn her eye downward, and scope the ground for more, making a low throaty sound. Grandma said she was quarreling, but I think chickens do that when they're content, like a kitten's purr.

We spent hours digging and feeding worms to Bitty, until her chest grew heavy and bulged with her feast.

Bitty had a respiratory condition somewhat like asthma in humans. She'd run around the yard huffing and puffing with her tongue hanging out just like old man Wallock, our neighbor, did after he walked up the small hill to the grocery store. There were no vets close by, and even if there were, we couldn't afford a doctor for a chicken.

I remember one hot spring day when Bitty was

sitting on her eggs in the nest she'd built inside an overturned wooden box by the fence. It was time for her to set and hatch babies, although we didn't even have a rooster. It was a natural thing for Bitty to do. While playing in the back room with Booze I heard a commotion in the yard. I slipped out the door and peered around the corner. Before me was a scene of madness. Grandma was beating Bitty across the back with the broom. The only other time I had ever seen her get that angry was once when Edward asked her to cook potatoes for him. But there was something wrong with them and he wouldn't eat them. I remember how she got an arm around his neck and nearly choked him as she pried his mouth open and stuffed those potatoes down his throat. I shivered as she slammed the broom down on poor Bitty once more. Bitty raced around the yard, her eyes wild, her mouth open and gasping for air, her tongue hanging out the side of her mouth, her wings flopping desperately, as she tried to fly through the dust and over the wire fence. I stood by the house, my hands over my mouth, trying not to scream. I couldn't move. Grandma swatted and beat that chicken until Bitty finally lay twitching in the yard among some weeds next to the fence. Grandma's eyes were crinkled into slits; her face was blood red, tight and twisted into a snarl. Her hair had fallen into her face, sweat ran down her cheeks onto her throbbing neck, and her breath came in short, ragged gasps.

Grandma turned a sharp eye on me. I jumped.

She inhaled quickly, and then she spit in the dirt and wiped her mouth with a trembling hand. "I won't have that thing acting like that around here," she said in a dark whisper and jerked her thumb at the nest box. Then she turned and stalked back toward the house billowing up dust with her heels as she stomped through the dirt and patches of grass. The door slammed behind her. Bitty's body heaved with each labored breath, her wings lax now and spread out. I picked her up, and her neck hung in a peculiar manner. I cradled her in my arms as I carried her to the back playroom and placed her inside a cardboard box on the floor. It had been like a scene out of a bad horror movie. Bitty looked like she was going to die. I got some water from the sink and sprinkled it on her head, then sat on the floor and gently stroked her feathers until her breathing became easy and she could raise her head. I didn't know what she had done to make Grandma so furious. I just knew it must have been something awful.

Bitty brought us many years of happiness.

Then one cold, rainy day, while Grandma was on her way to the post office, Edward and I spotted Bitty flopping around in the back yard in distress. We rushed outside, scooped her up and brought her inside. Her bill hung open as she fought for air, and her breath came in tight wheezes. We didn't know what to do. Grandma always rubbed Vicks salve on our necks when we had a cold. We grabbed the jar of Vicks Vapor Rub, slathered it up and down Bitty's neck, and laid her in front of the heater, hoping for a cure. Alas, our efforts failed. We stroked her feathers until she died.

When Grandma returned we told her what had happened. Her stern face took on a sad look. We gathered a box and an old towel, carefully wrapped Bitty in the towel, gingerly laid her in the box, and buried her at the edge of the garden, with a rock for a headstone.

We all cried.

*

One morning when Booze was about a year old, I was playing with her in the back room. We were wrestling on the floor, having fun, me giggling, delighted to have a real live dog to entertain me during those long days alone in that back room.

Booze rolled and tumbled, yelping in pure joy. I sat up and she wrapped her front paws around my arm just as Grandmother came into the back room. "What are you doing?" An angry tone edged her voice. "Vulgar! Vulgar acts with that dog?" Pain shot through the left side of my head. I heard bells and red and purple stars flashed before my eyes. The light was fading. I was trying to hold onto the world but being pulled away, and everything faded into blackness. The next thing I knew Grandma had my head under the faucet at the sink. I cried and screamed and knew all the neighbors must have heard. The pain in my head pulsed with my heartbeat. I finally sat down on the cold floor. Water dripped from my hair and ran in streams down into my eyes and onto my shirt. Grandma grabbed the broom and swatted Booze across the back, bending her to the floor. Booze tucked her tail between her legs, let out a yelp of surprise, and bolted out the door.

"You're not to have that thing in the house ever again." A fist clamped inside me. I was totally confused. I didn't even know what that word *vulgar* meant, but I knew it must have been really bad. I didn't figure out until many years later what had set her off. The dog was humping my arm.

Jenny Sturgill

*

The weeks stretched into months, then years. Booze grew into a medium sized mutt with a tea colored coat that shone in the sunlight. She had white spots that feathered across and between her toes and her wet black nose wiggled at the scent of the table scraps we fed her. We couldn't afford dogfood, but she seemed healthy, her eyes were bright and shiny, like clean glass. She and I spent many days playing house under the porch. Booze was more than willing to get wrapped up in a blanket and be my little girl or sit quietly and patiently as I taught her her ABC's and read to her from my books. Other times she was a ball of energy running around the yard, chasing after her tail just because it was there. She made me laugh with her silliness. She was sweet as chocolate cake and when I hugged her she felt soft and fluffy and muscular. She was the only friend with whom I could share my deepest secrets and know she would not tell anyone. Needless to say Booze never became a mother, not with a guardian like Grandma and a tight fence around our yard.

After a few years she developed what looked to be breast cancer. Her breasts hung under her belly, raw, with open, oozing sores, and Grandma decided to put her down. She asked our neighbor across the fence to do the job. Mr. Meadows came to the door the next day. He was a flat-bellied man with a thin face and white teeth. His shirt sleeves were rolled up and he had a rope wrapped around his bony wrist, a shotgun tucked at his side. I watched from inside the window as he called Booze to him and tied the rope around her neck, tugged her out the gate, and up the road. She walked behind him with her tail tucked between her legs and her head bent as if she knew the outcome would not be good. The warm weather was here and the trees had grown leaves all up and down the river bank. They disappeared down through the towering trees and brush to the rippling stream, out of sight.

    I pressed my nose against the window and felt my lips quiver. My shoulders shook as I cried silent tears, damp against the window. The shot rang out. I jumped and fresh tears squeezed out between my lids. Mr. Meadows climbed back up the bank with the empty rope in his hand. I went out into the yard and picked up Booze's dish, a discarded tin pie plate, and held it close to my chest. In the house I gently placed it in the garbage pail. I missed Booze, even though she had grown old and didn't play as much as she once had. She had given me many hours of happiness throughout the years. I think Grandma missed her, too.

Jenny Sturgill

Words to Live By

My most vivid memory, growing up in a rural community of Kentucky in the late 1950s, was my first day of school--the day I quit.

I was seven years old. I awoke early that day, eager for streaks of light to enter the window above the broken-down couch where I slept. I'd marked off the days on the calendar ever since that man came and spoke with Grandma.

I jumped out of bed, rummaged through my dresses, and picked my best and cleanest old dress. In front of the mirror, I brushed my tangled brown hair, and caught a glimpse of Grandma watching me. Our eyes locked.

"Can you brush the back, Grandma?" I asked, handing her the brush. She was already drinking, I could smell it on her breath.

Grandma's drunken binges came on as sudden and furiously as the thunderstorms we got on hot August days. This morning she looked older than her age. Her mouth was lined with wrinkles, her shoulders stooped from the weight of her life. At times I'd find her, head cradled in her hands, weeping. I wanted to reach out, but no one could penetrate the curtain she'd pulled tightly around her. I took a deep breath and said, "Grandma, why don't you want me to go to school?"

"It's nonsense. You, getting all high and mighty, people snooping around here," she said.

"The truant officer said you'd get in trouble, remember?"

Grandma gave my hair one last tug and hurled the brush against the wall. In the corner a mountain of dirty clothes tumbled to the floor. Dead silence filled the room.

Anticipation overtook me and my steps quickened as I headed out the door toward the foot bridge. It swayed and buckled with each step, planks missing, sometimes two in a row, a long jump for seven-year-old legs. The sight of the river below--cold, deep, and greedy--sent a chill through me as I hurried across.

No bigger than a house, the one room school sat at the woods' edge between walls of trees. The schoolyard was crowded with children laughing and frolicking with delight. A little girl twirled around and around, her skirt standing out from her waist like an open umbrella. Jealousy stabbed me, and I placed my hand over the torn pocket on my faded dress.

Jenny Sturgill

The teacher with a quick smile stood in the doorway, her hair pulled back and tied in the back with a white ribbon. She wore sensible shoes, and a crisp blue dress pinned at the throat with an old-fashioned brooch. She ushered us inside.

The blackboard stretched across the front wall. Four rows of seats lined the middle of the room, one row for each grade, one through four. Over to the side of the room, next to the teacher's desk, stood a pot-bellied stove. A hint of last year's burnt coal still lingered in the air.

After the morning activities, the teacher handed us our first-grade readers. The book felt firm and slick, filled with brightly colored pages, and held stories about a little girl and boy. I beamed with delight. I'd never seen such a fine book. I couldn't wait to show Grandma and Edward. Since Edward was five years older than me, he had taught me to read. I slipped it inside my book bag.

I savored every minute of the day, until...

"One of our readers is missing," the teacher said, busy putting things away. "Everyone please look for it." Feet shuffled, papers rattled. I sat as still and white as a stone.

"Ok," the teacher said, "everyone open your book bags."

My heart pounded against my chest, I could hardly breathe, and I felt myself shaking. I removed the book and handed it to her, and I felt piercing eyes burning holes through me. I bolted out the door, raced down the hill, across the bridge, all the way back to our little ramshackle house.

I found Grandma lying in a twisted tangle of dingy sheets, a half-empty bottle of Old Crow on the table beside her bed.

"I quit, I hate it," I said.

"Good," she said, in an unnatural tone, then turned over to face the wall.

I walked to the porch, leaned against the post, and sobbed. Tears trickled down my cheeks and dripped onto the floor, making little circles like sprinkles of rain.

Days passed. Grandma sobered up. Nothing interested me, not even my frayed, dog-eared books that I'd looked at a hundred times.

Every day, my friend Charlotte told me about her school day. We'd sit in the tall grass, scoot as close as we could to each other, and talk, the wire fence between us. Grandma always built a fence around every place we lived, either to keep me in or keep the world out, perhaps both.

"Go back, it's fun," Charlotte said, her blue eyes

dancing.

I knew I had to go. Besides I didn't want trouble for Grandma.

The first day back, I hung close to the woods until the last child entered the door. Then I eased inside, hiding my soiled hands in the folds of my skirt.

"Glad you're back," the teacher said, handing me my book.

Sunshine reigned, but the day soon ended. The teacher pulled me aside and said,
"Jenny, I'd like to speak with you."

My heart leaped in my chest. I could hardly breathe.

"Because you can read, tomorrow, I'm going to have you sit in the second grade row. Is that okay with you?"

I nodded, my cheeks on fire, doubt welling up inside of me. She smiled and gave my hand an understanding squeeze. The book wasn't even mentioned. "Jenny," she said to me, "always hitch your wagon to a star, and if you make it halfway you'll be doing extremely well."

From that day until this, my life has been driven by those words, spoken by a teacher sitting in a wooden chair on a bare floor, in a one-room school in the mountains of Kentucky.

The Bridge

Hard rain peppered the window panes for more than two weeks. The ground sucked at our shoes and water ran off the mountains in huge streams, carrying twisted and interlaced mats of timber down to the roads, stopping traffic. People gathered on higher ground, seeking refuge in all the houses that weren't in danger from flooding. Even Grandma opened her doors to the neighbors. The house buzzed with strange voices. We had moved into a house that sat on a high bank, and the back part of it projected high above the ground, but even so, the water inched dangerously closer to the back of our home. The space under the house was only used for storage. I pressed my nose against the window and watched as the water crept nearer and nearer. The swollen river was a muddy mass that seethed with houses, trees, and dead animals. Homes were ripped from their foundations and crushed like eggshells. I watched from the window as the water rose over the old footbridge and took it down.

How was I going to get to school with the bridge gone? I loved school and my heart saddened at the thought of missing any days. I'd need a boat to cross over to the other side. The school was across the river and up on the side of the mountain, a long walk for any ten-year-old child. What was I going to do with my time? I didn't know when the bookmobile would ever be able to come back. I loved to read and it passed the time for me. My heart skipped a beat at the thought of having to stay home for a long time with nothing to do.

The water never rose high enough to make us evacuate. The rain stopped, the clouds parted, and the sun shone again. The river soon retreated back into its banks, but it left thick mud behind. Seven or eight inches of the smelly stuff covered peoples' floors, their furniture, and any belongings that hadn't been stored up high. Women spent days washing their bed quilts and clothes. It took several washings to get the mud out. Our neighbors carried their meager furnishings out onto their lawns to dry in the sunlight, and then began the laborious task of trying to shovel the thick mud out of their houses. The Red Cross came, and some people received new furniture. Some didn't.

The bridge, what remained of it, dangled from both sides of the riverbank, hanging down into the water.

"How long will the bridge be out, Grandma?" I

Against the Wind

took a spoonful of oatmeal and twirled it around inside my mouth. Grandma turned around from the stove, frowning. "It'll be a long time. May as well get used to it." My shoulders slumped and I pushed the bowl of oatmeal away from me. I didn't feel like eating anymore. "Could someone take me in a boat?" I looked up at Grandma and felt a grain of hope sprout.

"No! You're not riding in no boat. Who'd want to take you, then come back every evening to get you?" she snapped. "Besides, you're liable to fall in and drown." My eyes blurred with tears. I blinked them away went into the bedroom that was my refuge during the day. I picked up my school books and thumbed through them. If I did a page every day, I'd stay caught up. The work was hard without a teacher, but I managed to keep up, somewhat.

Soon they started to work on the bridge. Every evening I'd look out the window to see how much progress had been made. First the cables were strung across the river, then they started laying the planks for the floor boards. My heart swelled with anticipation. When they had most of the boards laid across, Grandma sent me to see how soon they'd be finished.

It was late in the evening when I made my way

up the road the short distance to the bridge. My heart speeded up and I felt a knot in my stomach as I approached the workers. I was shy about talking to strangers, but Grandma had told me what to say. Lumber and wires were strewn across the ground, but I could see that the planks that made up the floor of the bridge were almost complete. As I approached, a short man walked toward me with a hammer in his hand, his shoes kicking up little puffs of dust. His eyes narrowed in the harsh sun and little beads of sweat popped up on his forehead. He was wearing a khaki jacket over olive green work pants. His belly hung slightly over his belt and he wiped his forehead occasionally with his wrinkled, dingy handkerchief.

"Hey mister, is the bridge almost finished?" I came a little closer to him. He had kind eyes and tilted his head to the side a little.

"We still have to put on the sides, but the floor will be done in a few days." He smiled a little half smile, and placed the hammer back in his tool box. It made a clanging sound as it hit the other tools. "How old are you?" he asked.

"I'm nine, and I go to Boldman School over there." I pointed to the white building that was barely visible through the trees on the side of the mountain. "I'm in the third grade. I haven't been to school since the bridge went out." He turned, shaded his eyes, and looked in that direction. "When will the sides be put on?"

"Honey, it'll be a long time before the sides are placed. I tell you what. If you want to start back to school when all the planks are done I'll walk with you and hold your hand all the way across." He grinned. The planks seemed awfully narrow, just barely wide enough for one person. I bit my lower lip and looked at the swollen, caramel-colored water below.

"I'll ask my Grandma. Thanks, mister." I hurried back down the road to our house.

Grandma was in the kitchen, cooking pinto beans on the stove. The scent filled the house. It was the scent of poor people, and it seeped out the windows and doors of many houses, ours included. I told her what the man had said. She opened the lid on the pot and took a spoon full of beans out, blew across them, placed the spoon to her lips, sucked in the soup, and grimaced. "No! That thing don't have sides on it, besides I don't want you messing around with no strange men." She waved me away and turned back to the stove.

"He said he'd hold my hand and he seems to be real nice. He said he'd be there in the evenings, too, to walk me back across." I stood with my hands clamped together, desperate for her to understand me. "Grandma, I've missed almost two months of school already. Will you just think about it?" I felt a lump gather in my throat. How I wished Grandma wouldn't be so difficult. Everything had to be a struggle. She didn't care if I got an education or not. She'd just as soon I never went back to school. She said I always had my nose in a book. What else was there to do? I couldn't have friends over and I wasn't allowed to go anywhere. Books took me places, wonderful exciting places, and school was such an inviting place to be. There I had friends, teachers who cared, and challenges every day. There was always something new and exciting to do.

  I worried for days as Grandma thought about it, nurturing my little ray of hope like a delicate flower. Then, finally, when my hope had all but faded away she said, "The boards are all across the bridge now, so I guess you can go on to school in the morning." All my tension drained away and an excitement rose through me.

  The next morning I was up and dressed, ready to go before the first light filtered under the shades. As soon as it was time, I quickly raced up the road to the edge of the bridge. The man was there, waiting as he had promised. He smiled broadly, his teeth large and stained by cigarettes. He reached out to me and I slipped my hand into his. His hand felt rough but solid and safe beneath my touch. We stepped onto the first few planks. The bridge lurched and jerked under our feet.

"What is your name?" he asked, walking slowly so I could keep up.

"My name's Jenny, and I live down there just to the left of the road." I gestured toward our house. The bridge moved, my heart speeded up, and I squeezed his hand. The further we walked, the more the bridge swung, rocked, and bucked. My fear squeezed my racing heart, but I held on tight to his hand. I looked down at the caramel colored water swirling below, cold, dark and ravenous, waiting to swallow anything that fell into its depths. Finally we reached the other side and I let go of his hand. "Thanks, mister," I called over my shoulder as I raced off to the bottom of the hillside, relief flooding my body.

Everyone was glad that I was back at school. The teacher hugged me and all the other students were thrilled to see me. The day was soon over and I found myself back at the edge of the bridge. The man wasn't there. I looked to the other side, but he wasn't there, either. My heart stopped and I felt terror racing up my spine. He had promised he'd be there. Grandma was right, I should have waited until the sides were completed to start back to school. I sat down on the ground. My heart hammered so hard I could feel it beneath my fingertips. The muddy water below looked angry and turbulent. Where was he? Tears turned to sobs. I put my head on my knees and wept. Grandma would be mad if I was late getting home. I had no choice but to try to make it back across, alone. I wiped the tears from my face with the back of my hand and stood up. I edged one foot onto the bridge. It started to wobble, and shake. There was nothing to hold onto. I screamed through clenched teeth, got down on my hands and knees and crawled. I felt as if I was being swallowed alive by a dark black hole. I willed myself not to look down at the violent, swirling water making its mad dash downstream. I crawled a piece and stopped. I just couldn't do this. I gulped air and shuddered, suddenly cold even though I could feel the sun's heat on my back. The bridge took a lunge. I lay down on my stomach and held on to the side of a plank with my left hand. My desperation grew. The movement got worse and worse and I heard the echo of footsteps. The next thing I saw were two work boots standing in front of my eyes. My eyelids flickered.

Against the Wind

The man thrust his hand out to me. I looked up to meet his steady gaze, and the sight of him reduced my fear. "I'm sorry, honey; I got tied up on the other side." He smiled and gave my hand a tight squeeze. "Always wait for me. I'll be here, just be patient."

I sort-of believed him. My tongue felt frozen. I set my jaw and trailed behind him across the wobbly bridge, holding tightly to his hand as he led me to safety. We reached the other side and I said goodbye and hurried on down the road to our house. Grandma was waiting in the door, her eyebrows tugged together. "Why are you so late?" She held the door open for me and I scooted past her.

"I had to stay and talk to the teacher," I lied. I wasn't about to tell her the man hadn't shown up or she wouldn't let me go to school until the bridge was completed. From that day forward the man was there every day, waiting for me on both sides of the river. He squeezed my hand one last time on the day that the bridge was complete. "Goodbye," he said. "The best of luck to you. Now you study hard. It's been my pleasure, Miss Jenny. I'll miss you." And he bowed.

"I'll miss you, too." My face stretched into a smile, and I turned and headed down highway 23 to home.

Jenny Sturgill

Becoming a Woman

Six months into my ninth year I became ill. Well, that's what I thought, in my nine-year-old mind. I had just started the fourth grade, my last year at the one room school across the river and up on the hillside. It was just an ordinary day with the sun shining outside and children at play in the neighborhood, their voices drifting up through the open back room window.

After using the rusty lard bucket we kept behind the door in the back room as a chamber pot, I looked down and saw blood in my underwear. My heart raced and fluttered in my chest like a bird, and panic clawed inside of me. Had I hurt myself somehow? There was no pain. I bent over and looked. Where had it come from? I screamed for Grandma to come quick. She hurried into the room with her hands still wet from washing dishes, swiping them up and down on the front of her flowered apron. "What's the matter? What's all that yelling about?"

I pulled down my underwear and showed her the bright red spot on my panties, looked away, and shifted self-consciously.

"Oh good Lord! That's what big girls are supposed to do!" Her face turned red and her lips stretched into a hard, straight line. She gave me a disgusted onceover, sucked in her breath, mumbling something I couldn't understand, and stalked out the door with her hands on her hips. I felt small and ashamed. Big girls? I wasn't big. Did she mean fat? I wasn't fat either. What was wrong with me? I wanted Grandma to sit down and explain. Terror filled my mind as I stared down at the round spot. My stomach hurt and tears gathered behind my eyelids.

That afternoon Grandma brought me some sanitary pads, threw them into the room and said, "Use these." Then she turned and walked out. After opening the box and reading the instructions I figured out what to do with them. Every time I used the pail I changed pads. I felt unclean and guilty, and they were all gone in no time. When I was out, I was too embarrassed to tell her I needed more, but finally I got up enough nerve to say something.

"What!" Her fists were back on her hips again. "You're out already? You can just do without." What would I do now? After a long pause, I went to the bedroom, pawed through the rag drawer, found a good sized rag, and stuck it in my pocket. Every time I felt wet I reached down in my pants and wiped, then stuffed it back in my pocket. In three days the bleeding stopped. Overwhelmed with relief, I put the incident behind me.

The days passed without any other sign. Then one day the red spot on my underwear was back. My heart raced as I stared at the spot. I'd thought I was cured. My sickness was back! I thought I was going to die, and I imagined facing my final unknown alone. I couldn't tell Grandma -- she got so angry at any mention of it. I didn't understand at all and there was no one I could confide in. I worried that everyone could tell, and my shoulders drooped as if I had the weight of the world on them. The body I saw in the mirror seemed new and strange and I was curious about what was happening. My emotions were strange, too, searing hot one minute and cold the next. I moped around the house doing nothing. I'd check every few hours to see if the blood was gone but it wasn't, there was just more of it. Good thing there were plenty of rags in the rag drawer. I found another one and stuck it in my pocket.

I had started to develop breasts and knew I needed a bra. I was too embarrassed to talk to Grandma about it, so I went into the rag drawer and made myself a bra out of some of them. I sneaked into the old trunk in the back room and took one of

Grandma's bras out for a pattern, and I hand-sewed it together. I didn't have a fastener for the back so I used a safety pin. When it got dirty I'd slip into the kitchen while Grandma was gone to the store, wash it, and hang it on a nail on the back of the house to dry. Grandma never went around the back of the house so she never did find out.

We were doing something at school one day that required us to get up out of our seats and move around. When I stood up I felt a gush between my legs. Oh no! I backed up into the corner and watched as everyone busied themselves with their projects, standing by their desks. The teacher had her back to the class, writing something on the blackboard. I had my rag, but I couldn't just wipe there in front of everyone, and I'd already used my morning bathroom break. My back was turned toward the wall. I took a quick look around the room and eased back as close to it as possible. Good, no one was looking. I quickly wadded my rag in my fist then reached down in the back of my pants, wiped as quick as a flash, and stuck it back in my pocket.

The more I bled the more worried I got. I'd lie on my couch bed and stare up at the ceiling and wonder how much longer I had to live. Would Grandma be sad? Would she miss me when I was dead? I didn't want to die, I wanted to become a journalist and make something of myself. I wanted to know everything. Then I'd fall asleep with a prayer on my lips.

The blood just kept happening. It would come, I'd get better and it would stop, and then it would come again. Since the bleeding wasn't heavy, I discovered that folded up tissue paper in my underwear provided enough protection to last from one bathroom break to the other so I got rid of the rag I'd carried in my pocket.

We weren't church going-people, and Grandma always said. "Look at those hypocrites going to church, hiding behind their religion." But I was able to sneak the black-and-white television over to a preaching station and listen. Every Sunday I'd listen to the preacher's words about Jesus and his healing power. He spoke with great passion and sensitivity, pointing to the heavens with an astounding hallelujah. I sat cross-legged on the floor and watched as he poured out his message. I think I always believed in God and His power to heal. The preacher would say, "Now folks, if there are any brethren or sisters out there that are suffering illnesses, just put your hand on the television, place the other one on the body part that you want to be healed, and God will heal you. Just do it, and let the Lord take away your sickness and afflictions." As he prayed I would place my one hand on the television and the other on my stomach. He'd make his voice deeper and pray, "Dear Heavenly Father take pity upon these suffering souls and heal them from their afflictions, Lord have mercy on them, let your power take hold and drag that hurt from them..." On and on he went, asking for healing. I sat there holding onto my stomach and the television with my eyes closed, and I knew that God had the power to do great things.

The bleeding stopped and I felt the burden roll off my shoulders and relief rush in. But then a few weeks later it returned. Had God changed his mind? I must have done something sinful for God to bring back the sickness again. I'd find myself again in front of the television, pleading with God to heal my sick body. I was unable to keep my mind on anything else except my pending death.

I managed to keep clean without any kind of protection except wadded tissue paper, but I was sure I had done something sinful. This went on for about a year, and in the meantime I changed schools. I now attended Harold Elementary School which was down the road past the post office, about a mile from our house.

Jenny Sturgill

I walked home with my friend, Judy, for lunch every day. We were the same age, but Judy was lucky. She had a good-natured Mom and Dad, and a loving family to take care of her. I'd met Judy when I started grade school at Harold. At recess I'd stayed by myself and hovered alone close to the side of the building. Judy came up to me one day and said, "Come, play jumprope with me." I smiled, took her outstretched hand, and we were friends from that day forward. We talked about everything, from how babies were born to sex. We shared all the thoughts and wonders of a couple of naïve nine-year-olds. I leaned on her for support. She had kind, chocolate-colored eyes, and long black hair that was shoulder length, with fresh bouncy curls. Her smile was bigger and brighter than anyone else's. She always was my encourager, telling me I was pretty and smart. She cheered on my every accomplishment. I wished I could spend the night with her so we could talk and whisper secrets over smooth pillowcases in the dead of the night. We both were curious about everything, especially boys and sex. She even found out about how people had sex and told me. I was shocked and we giggled and vowed to each other to never do that. Every time we saw a pregnant women Judy would say, "Just think, she's done it." We'd laugh and say we would be ashamed to go out of the house in that condition, announcing to the world what we'd been up to. Sometimes we were just comfortably quiet together, when we didn't have something new to talk about.

*

It was a bright spring day with bird songs in the air and the sun was high in the sky. I noticed how it glistened off Judy's hair. I envied her those beautiful tresses. As we came out of the post office Judy looked at me and said in a bright and bubbly voice, "Your hair is shiny, that means you're healthy."

With a solemn face I grabbed hold of Judy's arms and turned her around to face me. "No I'm not! There's something terribly wrong with me. I'm sick and going to die!" I blinked back tears and my voice came out shaky. I felt the blood drain from my face, as I struggled to contain my emotion. Judy stopped and took my arm, her eyes grew round and expectant, and her brows rose, as if she were trying to make sense of what I was saying. She stared at me with such disbelief as we faced each other, and I felt a tear slip down my cheek.

"What's wrong with you?" She gave me a tight hug. We rocked back and forth, and I smelled the scent of strawberry shampoo in her hair. My eyes blurred with tears. "I'm bleeding...you know...down there. It goes away then comes back." I looked down at my feet. "I'm afraid I'm going to die." Judy pushed back away from me.

"Oh, no you're not!" She pushed my hair away from my face, and looked me in the eye, and then started walking up the road. "You're not going to die, my sister does that. It's normal, all girls do it. Mother buys her pads to use. It only lasts a few days then stops, and it comes every month, but I haven't started mine yet." She grinned. "It's called 'having your period.'" She tugged on my arm and spoke in a quiet, lighthearted tone.

"I thought you had to be fat." I sniffled.

"No, no, Jenny, every girl does it. It's so they can have babies, somehow." She screwed her face into a question and shrugged, then paused at the top of the steps that led down the hill to her house. "Don't worry Jenny; you're not going to die." We both laughed.

I let out a breath, and the most blessed sensation rushed over me as I walked on up the road to my house. I felt well and strong, and full of new hope for the future. My feet were light, and I walked with a giddy step the rest of the way home.

Rising Water

When I was ten years old the icy rain fell from the sky once again for the better part of the week. It poured off the roof in sheets until the river spilled over onto the dry land, turning the thick dust to thicker mud. Once more, coffee-colored water crept inch by inch up our yards, coming dangerously close to the foundations of our homes. Streams gushed off the mountains, tumbling rocks and small bushes down to block roads and fill the river with debris.

I sat at the kitchen table reading my library book. Placing my thumb between the pages I closed the book and studied Grandma as she hovered over the stove. She looked so much older than her given years. The pale blue dress she wore was unbecoming to her, and had come from one of the packages of clothes that my aunt sent us. It was buttoned all the way to the throat. A frayed print apron covered the front and she wore low-cut, black, comfortable shoes. Her gray hair was secured at the crown with a comb. A few strands escaped it and fell loose to frame her square chin.

In her hand she held a sun-bleached stick with which she stirred the wash that was boiling in a large pot on top of the stove. She boiled and bleached all our underwear and socks until the elastic was gone, fearing that normal washing might leave a germ lurking. She paused and laid the stick next to the burner and looked at me. "The rain has stopped for now. I want you to hurry to the post office and get my mail. I'm expecting a check." Her mouth was tight. Silence fell, leaving unspoken words hanging in the air. I knew better than to refuse to go, even though I shuddered at the thought of such a long walk in such bad weather.

I laid my book on the seat of my chair and took my thin twill jacket from its back. I eased my arms through the sleeves and stepped out into the thick mist, breathed in the scent of the wet earth, and looked up at the dark sky that was still filled with low, hovering rain clouds. I shivered as the cold wind blew down my collar and around my neck. Then I wadded the collar up in my fist and forced my legs to hurry down the road. My grandmother's life hung on the door of the post office. She was dependent on checks sent to her from her children and the small government check to make ends meet.

It was about a mile each way down a two lane road to the post office. On the other side of the road rose great mountains. I'd walked that road every day for many years, through all kinds of weather, as I came home from school at lunch time each day to deliver the mail. Our lunchtime at the grade school was forty-five minutes long and I'd calculated the time down to the last minute. It took twenty minutes to walk each way and I had five minutes to eat my lunch, which consisted of a peanut butter sandwich and a glass of milk.

Worry overtook my mind. I had a real fear of water. I couldn't escape the memories of walking to school across that footbridge, the river an angry serpent below, snapping at me and thrashing its tail against the eroded banks.

I'd walked about halfway when I came to a place in the road where the muddy water lapped across it almost to the other side. The early spring cold raised goose-bumps along my legs and arms. I crossed to the other side of the road to walk on the dry pavement. It wasn't until later that I realized just how scared I was. If the water rose while I walked the other half-mile to the post office I'd be trapped and wouldn't be able to make it back home. A fleeting thought entered my mind, a wishful thought. I could stay with my best friend, Judy, until the water went down. That thought didn't last long. I might have only been ten years old but I was smart enough to know that Grandma would have a fit if I couldn't get back. I willed my feet to walk faster and raced on past Judy's house, not stopping at the top of the steps that led down to her house to see if she wanted to walk with me the rest of the way.

I glanced at her house as I hurried past. Our house was like a box with linoleum floors covering squeaky boards and dingy, painted wood walls. How I envied Judy her home and her nice parents. I dreamed about having a bedroom with a slanted attic ceiling, a canopy bed trimmed with lace, and wallpaper with tiny pink blossoms, like Judy did. Judy's mother was always sweet to me, offering me cookies on my brief stays, treating me like one of her own. I loved her house with the big cool porch that came complete with a painted green swing and comfortable chairs. The house was always filled with the buttery cinnamon smells that reminded me that this was a real home, even if I could only share it briefly. The whole atmosphere there was of love and peace. If Grandmother knew I stopped there I'm sure I'd get a lickin'. That was one of her oddities. She didn't want me to visit any of my friends and she'd never allow anyone to come to my house to play.

I trudged on down the road. The wind had picked up and the chill cut through my thin jacket as it whipped around my waist in a tight knot. There were no cars on the road today, so I had the pavement all to myself. On each side of the road, the soupy mud ran deep and my shoes stuck each time I stepped off the concrete.

I walked on past the general store run by Mrs. Sturgill, a kind, plump woman with a smile that spread wide and broadened until she was laughing. I could hear her chuckle even from outside the double green doors that faced the road. In the back of the store Mrs. Sturgill prepared and sold sandwiches and soft drinks at lunchtime. The storefront was cracked and smeared with age. I paused and stared at the checkerboard window, where jars of goodies smiled an invitation to "just try one." Pink mounds of bubble gum filled one jar, another overflowed with red and white sticks of peppermint candy. My mouth watered, and I could taste peppermint and horehound. How I wished I had money for a candy from those jars. Above the door a glass sign read, *Coca Cola*.

Down the road from the store was the post office. The stones that made up the structure were as gray as a December sky. The two half-shaded windows were like sleepy eyes, half-closed in slumber. I twisted the doorknob that was surrounded by many smudged fingerprints and gently gave it a shove. The door rattled open. Inside, the scent of paper mingled with the musty smell of decay. On the right a wall held rows of private mailboxes. Grandma didn't have a box of her own. Beside the mail boxes was a small window. I stretched on tiptoes to reach it.

"Any mail for Grandma today?" I asked Mrs. Cecil, the post mistress. A tall woman who wore a maroon top and loose fitting blue pants, sensible shoes, and glasses, she presided over the falling-apart post office. She stepped up to the window and removed her glasses. "I'm sorry but the mail train was late today. The train is in, over across the river, but the truck has to be loaded and brought over and then the mail has to be sorted."

I looked out at the dark clouds and thought about the rising water. Grandma would be mad if I didn't wait for the truck. I decided to go on down to the Texaco station just below the post office. Two red gas pumps stood in the center of a sea of concrete in front of the dingy white station. The owner was sitting on an upturned pop case just outside the door. His nails were chipped and stained black with engine oil, his knuckles scraped. The cuffs of his red flannel shirt were frayed and his clothes smelled of dust, oil, and gasoline. A cigarette hung from his lower lip and bobbed up and down when he talked. He was a war veteran, a school teacher, and had owned the station ever since I could remember. Often men gathered there to talk over politics and the weather, and tell lies. Stacked along a metal shelf were a few cans of oil and a box of fuses. The service rack was empty that day, and tools were scattered around the greasy concrete floor. A chamois, beyond further use, lay crumpled in the corner. Squatted in the opposite corner was a rusty drum filled with discarded boxes, used spark plugs, and crumpled paper towels stained with oil. Old discarded tires lined the side of the building. I sat down on a pop case.

"What are you doing so far from home in such bad weather?" He mashed out his cigarette against the concrete with his high-topped boot.

"I'm waiting on the mail truck." I leaned forward and craned my neck toward the bridge.

"I hear the river's rising over the road up toward your way." He gestured and I felt my heart speed up.

Just then I saw the mail truck come over the bridge and head up the road.

I jumped up and ran back up to the post office, where I stood outside the tiny window and felt the tension creeping up my spine. I paced back and forth and hesitantly popped my head up, watching as Mrs. Cecil sorted the mail. I'd been gone such a long time. I swallowed hard. Mrs. Cecil looked up from time to time and gave me a halfhearted smile. She finally cocked her head sideways with an apologetic look. "I'm sorry there's no mail for you today." My shoulders slumped.

As I stepped out the door, cold rain hammered my face. The wind now whistled around tree trunks and stirred up dead leaves that whirled around my feet. I was blinded by my long brown hair whipping into my face as the wind pushed me forward. It hurled icy rain from the pitch black sky as it swept along the mountains, tall trees bending so far down I could hear the limbs cracking. Water dripped down my face from my wet hair and my thin coat was soon soaked from the downpour. I sloshed through puddles that came up over top of my shoes. They made a squishing sound with each step. By the time I got to the place in the road where the water was rising, I was chilled to the marrow. The swollen spring waters churned against the mountain and completely covered the road!

I was paralyzed with fright. My whole body trembled, and I slumped and closed my eyes. I would have to wade across to get to the other side. I stood at the edge of the hungry water as panic overwhelmed my body. Grandma would be mad enough that I was wet and there was no mail. I had no choice but to wade through it. The water came almost to my knees and the cold was startling on my legs as I stepped into it. My vision blurred with unshed tears and I bit down on my lower lip to keep from crying. I felt like I was sliding down a steep cliff clutching at small bushes and branches and coming up empty-handed. I could barely keep upright. I couldn't tell where the road was. The water was getting deeper. It sloshed and rippled around my legs as I struggled against the waves, my feet and legs heavy as logs.

    I took a panicked breath, stood still, and looked around. I had gotten off course. I had to make it back to the edge of the road and follow the mountainside. Finally I came to a place where the water was shallow, and my eyes fixed on the pavement beyond. My heart pounded and I gulped air. Tension drained from me as I pulled my feet out of the water. I shivered with cold. The water ran down my legs and into my shoes. I felt as drained as a dead battery. I could feel my skin shriveling inside my socks, my teeth chattered, and I blew warm breath on my numb fingers.

    Grandma's face was visible in the window as I

Jenny Sturgill

approached the house, her brow furrowed, her face pressed against the glass. I stepped through the door. "You didn't get any mail," I said, holding out my palms.

I was met by a questioning stare. "What took you so long? Where've you been laying out at, all this time!" She spoke through gritted teeth, her jaw tight, her words loud and accusing. She raised her hand and I flinched. Then she let her arm drop to her side.

"I had to wait for the mail, and the water was over the road." My voice came out breathless and shaky. I straightened my spine and brushed past her to the small heater that sat at the opposite end of the room and stood in front of it to dry myself. I heard the squeak of the floorboards under my feet. as Grandma stalked off into the kitchen. I pulled off my jacket and hung it on the back of the chair, changed into dry clothes and picked up my library book, which was still lying in the seat. I couldn't wait to dig back between the pages of this comforting story to read about a prince and princess who lived in a clean bright castle surrounded by a dense forest, and find out all about their delightful adventures on their white horses. I was already looking forward to visiting the bookmobile for the next book in the series.

The Janitor

I was eleven years old when I stood on the little balcony outside the grade school side door where the steps led down to the concrete pad that connected the lunch room to the school. The janitor was down there sweeping. The wind stirred up the leaves around his feet and I winced as I ran my fingers through my tangled hair. I looked down at him. He was a big man and walked with a limp. He had brown hair and little beady eyes that looked out from under thick bushy eyebrows in a way that made your blood run cold. His smile was big, but it was a knowing smile, not really a happy smile. It was more of a smirk, and his hands were large and groping. His belly hung over his belt in rolls of fat.

He looked up at me and poked me in my breast with the broom handle, acting as if he was trying to tickle me but I knew exactly what he was doing. I'd heard the other girls talk about him. It hurt. I knocked the broom out of his hands and he stood looking up, grinning that smirky grin. My face was hot and I felt embarrassed and guilty. I turned around and went back into the school building. After taking my seat in Mrs. Akers' class. I leaned over and whispered to my friend, Sharon, "You better stay away from Mr. Harrington. He poked me in the boob."

Her eyebrows rose and she nodded. "I know, he does that to all us girls." Sharon had short brown hair and thick lips that stretched into a smile that lit up her whole face. She had a funny giggle in her throat that made you want to giggle along with her. Sharon and I always had something to talk about and she could say the funniest things about something or somebody. She could take the most serious situation and turn it around to make it sound lighthearted.

Janet placed her elbows on the desk and leaned in. "What's going on? I need to know, too." Just then Mrs. Akers announced the start of class. I heard the sound of feet shuffling and papers rattling as everyone settled down into their seats, and silence settled over the room for a moment. I didn't tell Grandma about the incident with Mr. Harrington, because she would say it was my fault and be mad at me.

One cold morning a few weeks later, I was in the cloak room. After sliding off my coat I reached up to hang it on the peg. I heard a rustling, saw a shadow behind me, and thought nothing of it since this was where everyone hung their coats. Then I felt a hand creep around and cup my breast. I turned around and looked up into Mr. Harrington's face. At first his expression was hard to read, dimmed by the shadows. He cocked his head to the side and grinned, his eyes caught mine, and I could smell his sour breath. He cupped his other hand over my other breast and gave them a squeeze. "Stop it!" I grabbed his arms and gave him a big shove that caused him to stagger on his lame leg, and I heard the clatter of wood against wood as his cane fell to the floor. I ducked past him and out the door. My face burned, my whole body trembled, and my stomach felt vaguely queasy. I'd heard the tales about Mr. Harrington, how he'd get you cornered and slide his hand up your skirt or act like he was trying to tickle you and let his hand travel to your boobs or any other place he could get to. I slumped against the door, took a deep calming breath, and headed down the hallway to Mrs. Akers' fifth grade class. From then on, every time I saw him I'd turn the other way. I'd wait until he wasn't around to hang up my coat, or I just carried it with me.

At home I approached Grandma with eager expectation. She was in the kitchen washing dishes in the wash pan beside the sink. "Grandma, you know the janitor at school? He puts his hands on us girls.

Today he came into the cloak room when I was hanging up my coat and touched me on the boob." My heart speeded up. I took a seat at the kitchen table waiting for her reaction. I hoped she would give me support, maybe sit down and tell me how to handle such situations. She might even report him.

"You better stay away from him! Don't you talk to him or encourage him in any way." Her voice chilled my blood, all angry as she turned around and put her hands on her hips. Her mouth was pursed, her forehead crinkled. I felt small and guilty. Why would she think I'd done something to encourage him?

"I don't encourage him, I'm hardly around him anymore. All the girls are afraid of him and they stay away, too." I sighed, looked down at the table, and folded my hands in my lap, then got up and walked to the back room. What kind of girl did Grandma think I was, anyway? I'd never do anything to encourage Mr. Harrington, with his bad breath and groping hands. It didn't make any sense to me. My skin prickled at the thought of his hands on my body.

I stayed away from Mr. Harrington as much as possible. I never knew why the parents didn't report him to the principal. Maybe that sort of thing was just tolerated. I never reported him because I was afraid I'd be blamed or they wouldn't believe me. I suppose every one else thought the same way.

Time went on.

It was washday for Grandma. After she boiled our underwear and socks on the stove, she would haul the wringer washing machine out onto the porch and carry water out to fill it. She did the whites first, then the colored clothes, using the same water. This was an all-day job and she was tired at the end of the day. Edward and I knew that on washdays we'd only get peanut butter and bread for supper. I felt sorry for Grandma on those days, but she'd be grouchy and hateful, and we knew not to cross her.

I came home from school that day just like any other day. Grandma was standing beside the door as I entered. I heard the crack as her hand smacked my cheek, saw stars as the pain flamed across my face. "What? What was that for? I didn't do nothing." My voice trembled and my cheek tingled. Tears blurred my vision, and I bit down on my lower lip to keep from screaming. I felt as if I'd had the wind knocked out of me.

"You...you little rip, you've been laying out in the basement with that janitor." She stood over me with her legs spread and her hands on her hips, her eyes narrowed into slits of fury. I put my hands over my head for protection. "Why? I have not!" My voice came out broken and loud.

"I saw dirty hand-prints under the edge of your shirt today. I know what you've been up to." Her voice so loud it pierced my ears, her face bright red, twisted, and ugly. She stalked off into the kitchen.

How did hand-prints get on the wrong side of my shirt? What shirt? As I sat there on the couch I wondered how in the world this could have happened and how could she even think that I'd be laying up in the basement with a dirty old crippled man. I could not imagine it. There had to be an explanation. I felt as if I was in a bad dream. I rubbed my temples trying to think of a reason. After Grandma had time to cool off I went back into the kitchen and stood in the doorway. I didn't know exactly what to say, but I couldn't let her think that of me.

"What shirt had dirt on the inside? I want to see it." I took a deep breath and waited for her to answer.

She went out on the porch and took down a white blouse that had elastic around the bottom from the clothes line She held it up in front of my face. "This one, it was this one." She wadded the shirt in her hands and threw it down on the table, then turned and stomped over to the window and stared out with her arms folded across her chest.

I picked up the blouse and held it up to me and smoothed out the wrinkles. I hated this blouse. It was a pain, always riding up. That was it! That was it! I felt my face stretch into a smile. "Grandma those prints you saw were mine, where I'm always pulling this thing down because it always rides up. I'm never wearing it again!"

She looked at me, and for a moment I could see all the way into her eyes and thought I saw understanding. I think she actually believed me. She turned away and slid her hands into the twin pockets of her apron. After awhile she took the blouse back outside and hung it back on the clothesline to dry. I never wore the blouse again.

Years went by, uneventfully. I stayed away from Mr. Harrington and he never bothered me again. I never thought much about him, actually, until I was reminded about him when I was in the eighth grade. I was approached by Charlotte. She was a good little girl who came from a Christian home. "Has Mr. Harrington ever touched you in places he shouldn't?" Her eyes brightened with my tiny nod. "He touched me, and I'm going to the principal and tell. Will you come with me?"

After all these years the memories of the time

in the cloak room weighed on me. "I will, but do you think they'll believe us?"

"My parents told me to report him." We marched to the principal's office and told him what had been going on all these years. We were greeted with cool politeness. After we left the principal called Mr. Harrington into his office, but he stayed on for several more years.

*

Some years later we heard that he and his wife were found shot to death in their house. I was shocked and wondered if he had groped the wrong person or maybe even raped a girl, and that girl's family took justice into their own hands. I never knew the circumstances. I just know he probably got what was coming to him.

Usher

I always liked school. I loved every part of it, even the scent of chalk, paper, and books that seemed to linger in the air.

Mrs. Brooks handed out the history tests that day in early spring. She paced back and forth, and up and down the aisle with a pencil stuck behind her ear. She looked at the floor as if studying some script written on it, her hands clasped behind her back. She was a fairly tall woman, with kind eyes and an absolute respect for all education. "When you're finished put the test on my desk on your way out," she said as she passed my desk. Ronnie Allen sat in front of me and was my biggest competitor. I stared at the back of his head and wondered if he was going to make an A on this exam. I had to score at least a 95 on this test to take the lead. I was in the seventh grade, and I didn't know then that it would be one of the most memorable years of my life.

It was a contest of sorts between the two of us. We wanted to see which one of us would make the best grades in the class. That person would get to walk down the aisle first to usher in the eighth grade graduating class. All year we'd struggled with the competition. Each of us studied just as hard as the other.

The next day I received my test back. I turned it face down, so I wouldn't see what I'd made right away. My hands shook as I sat and looked at the blank page staring up at me. I finally picked up the corner and quickly turned it over. There on the top was 90 written in bright red pencil. I was a dead duck. I still hadn't taken the lead. I'd peeked over Ronnie's shoulder and saw the big red 95 on his paper. There was another test the following week, and I'd have to study extra hard for it.

My grandma didn't like my studying. For some reason known only to her, maybe she thought I'd get too smart, too big for my britches, as she always said. I never questioned her. That's just how it was. Each night after she went to bed I sat up on the faded brown couch I slept on and studied by the dim light that shined through the window from the porch light that Grandma kept burning all night. I studied long into the night that following week.

*

Once again Mrs. Brooks handed out the test papers. My heart speeded up as I turned it over and saw the first question. I didn't know that one. On to the second question. The blood drained from my face and I felt my heart beating against my chest. I didn't know that one, either. I slumped and tears made everything blurry. But then I took a deep calming breath and sat up straight. I went back to the first question. Maybe I could guess and get lucky. I finished the test, walked up front, and placed it on Mrs. Brook's desk. I really did want to win.

The day finally came for the announcement of who would be the usher for the eighth grade graduation. I held my breath. "We've decided to pick the girl *and* boy who have the highest grades to be ushers together." Mrs. Brooks rose from her seat, holding a clipboard in her hand. She put on her glasses, which hung from a chain around her neck, and held the clipboard in front of her eyes. "I'm proud to announce that the girl is Jenny Stumbo and the boy is Ronnie Allen." She stepped from behind her desk, walked back and stood beside our chairs. With a gleam in her eyes she said, "I'm so proud of you two."

I leaned forward in my chair, clasped my hands to my chest, then reached out and patted Ronnie's back. He looked back, his eyes dancing, sparkling and shiny. He grinned from ear to ear. "Congratulations." I smiled as I said it, my voice bubbly and light.

That evening I practically danced home. I couldn't help grinning to myself. Maybe Grandma would be proud of me this time. Maybe she'd let me study as long as I needed.

Maybe she wouldn't be drunk.

I went to the kitchen to tell Grandma my good news. "I've been chosen to be the usher for the eighth grade graduation." I threw my shoulders back, beamed, and laid my books on the kitchen table. Grandma was standing by the sink, washing dishes. Her hair was uncombed and she looked as if she'd just crawled out from under a rock. She dried a plate and placed it over the sink on an open shelf, then twirled around on her heel, staggering, almost falling. I could see that she had been drinking again. "When is it?"

"It's Friday night, two weeks from now." Panicking, I scanned her face and felt the dread creeping up my body.

"You can just tell them to find someone else. You've got no business traipsing up and down the road after dark. You're not going." I was always traipsing around doing something I ought not be doing, according to her. So far it hadn't been much fun. She had a way of fixing her eyes on you that made you want to disappear, especially when she had been drinking. She dried her hands on the dish towel and slammed it down on the counter, then brushed past me into the living room. I stood still, her words closing around me tighter than barbed wire. I went into the bedroom, leaned against the wall, and slid down. I sat there for a while, knees drawn to my chest, my head cradled in my hands. My mind raced. I should have known she'd pull something like this. She was a forceful woman. Her power was overwhelming and not to be questioned. I was desperate for her to understand, but she didn't seem to care if I succeeded at anything. I sometimes wondered if she *wanted* me to fail. Grandma always deviated from the norm. Simple things that other people just let pass them by were a big issue with her. I took a deep, calming breath and marched back into the living room. "Grandma I really worked hard for this," I pleaded, my arms open, palms up, my voice quivering. "I really want to go!"

"You just want people to brag on you, that's all. You'll never amount to anything. You're not going." Her direct gaze traveled slowly up and down my body, her lips tight. Her eyes narrowed and bored into mine. I turned and bit my lip to keep from shouting how much I hated her at that moment. I went into the living room, and lay down on the sofa. The tears that ran down my cheeks had waited a long time to come. I didn't know what to do. I wanted to make something of myself in spite of the Grandma's sneering predictions. Just once, I wished she could rejoice in my accomplishments. I wanted her to be proud of me.

The next morning I saw Mrs. Akers, my previous fifth-grade teacher, in the cloak room, a small room off of the hallway that led from the front door. She drew me close and I breathed in her aroma. She smelled clean, like soap and honeysuckle. She was a kind lady, in her mid-fifties. She had parchment skin seamed with fine wrinkles, but her green eyes were alert and intelligent, and her silver hair was smooth and shiny, swept back from her face in waves that gathered handsomely at the crown of her head. She once told me she would like me to come be her little girl. I wanted to stay close to her forever. She gave me a squeeze, cupped my chin in her hand and lifted my face to hers. "I'm so proud of you, Jenny." She smiled into my eyes.

"I can't go. Grandma said I had no business traipsing up and down the road in the dark." My throat was tight and my voice had a squeaky sound. I fought back tears, the way I always did when I felt like crying but didn't want to. I held my breath and said in my head, "*stop it, stop it,*" and the tears went away. It worked every time. Well, almost every time.

Mrs. Akers' smile faded from her face. I saw was confusion in her eyes, and her voice came out loud. "You can't go? That's ridiculous! This is a coveted honor! I can't believe she won't let you go."

"It's no use." She doesn't change her mind once it's made up." I hung my jacket on the peg next to Mrs. Akers' shawl.

"I just can't believe it. I'm so sorry, Jenny." Her voice had tears in it, and she had a faraway look in her eyes.

The bell sounded and I went on to class.

The next morning Mrs. Akers passed me in the hallway. She took my arm and pulled me aside. "Come to my room after school today...I have something for you," she said in a matter-of-fact way.

What could she possibly have for *me?* I couldn't wait until the last bell rang. I hurried down to Mrs. Akers' room, past students with notebooks in hand sauntering about the hallways, chatting in groups, waiting for their buses to arrive. I stood outside her door until the last child was gone, then I walked past empty chairs and stood in front of her desk. She looked up and smiled, opened the top drawer, took out an envelope, and handed it to me. On the front was Grandma's name, handwritten. "Take this home and give it to your Grandma. Don't open it, just hand it to her. Make sure she gets it. Okay?" My eyes widened and my mouth dropped open. "Okay, I will." I took the envelope and tucked it between the pages of my history book.

"Don't lose that, Jenny." A glimmer seemed to pass through her eyes.

My heart swelled with hope. On my way home I kept checking to make sure the envelope was still tucked inside my book, even though I'd only checked it a few minutes before. Grandma'd probably be mad that I'd told Mrs. Akers about her saying no. I wouldn't put it past her. She hadn't been sober since the middle of last week and she was so much meaner when she was drunk. I felt my heart speed up as I approached the door to our house. Grandma was in the kitchen, stirring a pot on the stove. She looked sober for a change. I fumbled to open the book, took out the envelope, and handed it to Grandma.

"What's this?" Her brow knitted into the slightest frown as she took it.

"Mrs. Akers said to give it to you." I turned, walked back into the living room and laid my books on the sofa. I peeked around the corner of the door and watched Grandma. She held the letter to the light then tossed it into the garbage without opening it. What was I going to tell Mrs. Akers and what did the letter say? It was just one more embarrassment. My shoulders drooped, and my chin trembled. I'd just stay home tomorrow, I couldn't face Mrs. Akers. Grandma returned to the stove. Her gaze wandered back to the trash. She walked over to the can and stared down at the envelope, then picked it up and studied the name. She slowly ripped it open. Her eyes widened, and she got a curious look on her face as she read the contents. Then she folded the paper and slid it into her apron pocket.

    I jumped back out of sight, tiptoed back into the living room, plopped down in a chair, and waited miserably for her reaction.

    The next morning Grandma stood by the stove as I ate my bowl of cereal. She turned to face the window, hesitating a long moment. "You can go to that thing you're in." Her voice came out a little high-pitched.

    My cheeks were glowing. I could feel my smile, and for an instant I felt the urge to hug her. It was only a fleeting thought. "Mrs. Akers said she'd give me a ride." My eyes flickered in her direction as I scooped up the last bite of cereal.

She twirled around and her voice turned lemon-sour as she stepped over to the table. "No, no, none of that! I don't want that busybody snooping around here! You can walk." Her eyes narrowed as her fingers brushed against the letter in her pocket. She looked down at her feet. I placed my dish in the dishpan, trying to hide my excitement. I brushed past Grandma, grabbed my books from the table and headed out the door. I couldn't wait to tell Mrs. Akers. I practically skipped my way to school that day.

Graduation day finally arrived. I couldn't wait for that night. I dressed in my pretty, navy blue dress with a white bodice and a belt around the waist. It had hung in the chifforobe so long that it was almost too small. When Grandma went to the store I'd try it on. I'd twirl in front of the mirror, smile, turn this way and that, and think how grand it would be to wear it to school, then I'd see Grandma coming and I'd quick put it back. When the time came to walk down the road to the school, I felt self-conscious, knowing that the whole neighborhood was watching from behind closed curtains. They weren't used to seeing me in a dress. Grandma always demanded that I wear pants.

Ronnie and I took our places in front of the

class. He looked over at me and smiled. "You look beautiful." Beautiful! Nobody ever called me beautiful before! He reached for my hand as the music started. "Isn't this just like walking down the aisle?" He gave me a mischievous grin. I floated along beside Ronnie as we ushered in the graduates.

Jenny Sturgill

Love Letters

Grandma had told me that I should never mess around with boys. If she got wind of it, she would wring my neck. I never thought much about it until I was fourteen-years-old and in the eighth grade. That's when I had my first boyfriend. That was Ronnie, my competitor for the top of our class. He was a head taller than me and always had his pants pulled up past his waist. His dark hair straggled onto his forehead, and smooth velvety skin. His eyes were a coffee brown and he could talk more than three or four people together. He lived down past the post office, across the bridge, and up on a hill. He had a sister named Linda who was younger, and I liked her a lot, too. She told me later that Ronnie had said he'd never get married if he couldn't marry me. I had known him since I started fifth grade at Harold. He had hinted that he liked me throughout the years, but I was either not interested or too naive to notice. Sharon and I talked about him and she would tell me things he said about me, such as how much he liked me and that I had nice hair. Sharon lived across the river, too, and I guess he saw her from time to time up at Mr. Conn's store, where everyone on that side of the river got their groceries. He'd been hanging around me for quite some time, talking, kidding around. I felt self-conscious around him and tried to avoid him, because I was having a problem with odor. Since we never took a bath I felt that I smelled. I didn't have deodorant and tried to wash with a rag as often as possible. I even went to the lengths of washing my underarms with Clorox. But that didn't work. I then smelled like bleach, and it made my skin peel off.

One time Mrs. Akers was going to have a class on hygiene. I worried for days about being embarrassed. I just knew that she was giving the class for my benefit. I hoped that it would be one of the days that Grandma found a reason for me to miss school. Seems like anytime there was something going on at school, such as a test or a play, she would send me to Pikeville on some errand that could have waited until Saturday. I liked going to town and wandering around the shops. I got to ride the city bus that had double seats on each side of the aisle, but the back row was for blacks. Over the seat was written "Colored Sit Here." The bus ran right in front of our house and dropped me off at my door. As it turned out she didn't make me stay home, even though I complained of a sore throat the morning of the class. I sat in my seat with my head down in Mrs. Akers' class that day. She went over personal hygiene with us. She said the odor was coming from the hormonal changes in our bodies, and it was important to keep ourselves clean by bathing every day. Grandma still wouldn't let me bathe, because she claimed I made too big a mess for her to clean up, even though I did all the cleaning up after myself now. We had nothing but a pan of water and a rag and to quickly wash up in the kitchen, with no privacy. My feet got so dirty that my ankles would be crusted over with what we called winter mange.

One time at recess, Ronnie and I were sitting on the benches in the little shelter by the school yard where students waited on the bus. We were alone. He leaned over and said, "You ever been kissed?" and looked down at his hands folded in his lap.

"No," I replied and felt the heat traveling up from my neck to my cheeks. "Wonder what it feels like?" He turned to face me and reached his arm around my shoulder. I stiffened. Grandma would kill me if she knew I was in the school shelter with a boy who had his arm around me. "Want to try it?" He leaned in, and I could smell the juicy fruit gum on his breath. He took his other hand and cupped my chin, pulling my face toward his. I closed my eyes and felt his lips press down on mine. They were soft and gentle. As if they had a mind of their own, my arms reached up and wrapped around his neck. A slow burning ignited in my chest. For a few seconds, I forgot about Grandma and her stern warning, then guilt washed over me and I pushed him away.

"I have to go."

"Why? The bell hasn't rung yet." He flinched back with a bewildered look on his face, shrugged, and his hands fell to his sides. I jumped up and ran into the school house, my face burning, my mind racing, overflowing with guilt. I couldn't look at him the rest of the day. I thought of the kiss and how gentle his lips had been against mine, and I'd felt a warm glow throughout my body. But still, I felt guilty. I was afraid that I'd committed a great sin and God would surely punish me. I went home and prayed.

The next day at recess we found ourselves back in the school-bus shelter. Ronnie reached for me but I pushed him away and pretended that I had to tie my shoe. He blinked, surprised, and his shoulders slumped. We talked about school and our ambitions. He told me he wanted to be an astronaut and work at Cape Canaveral. We discussed everything except our now-changed relationship.

We sat in that little shelter every recess the rest of the year. He tried to kiss me but I'd always push him away. We held hands but that was as far as it went. When school was out he'd come to meet me under a shade tree below where Rick Hale lived, up on a hill above the road. Rick was a smart boy with a big head and big bones. He'd wait for me to come down the road at lunchtime, and he'd run out and walk with me to school. I never thought of him as a boyfriend, but later on I learned he wanted to marry me. We always had a good time chatting away about anything and everything. I never knew he had a crush on me. When we grew up he asked me, "Did you think I just happened to come out the door whenever you walked by?"

I'd see Ronnie standing there in the shade waiting for me and my heart would speed up.

He'd reach for me with eager expectation. expecting a hug, but without meeting his eyes, I'd push him away. It was a hot summer and I could feel the sweat dripping down my face onto my neck and rolling between my breasts. My clothes were sticking to me from all that walking, and my face burned with the heat. I didn't smell very good. If he got a whiff of me I would be so embarrassed. My face got even hotter. He looked bewildered each time I pushed him away. There was confusion in his eyes, even sorrow. I really was flattered and I didn't know exactly how I felt. I liked him and wanted him to come meet me, but I had drawn a line around myself that I wouldn't let him cross. Finally he quit coming and started sending me letters.

The postmaster handed me each letter through the little window. I opened the letter and read it. He confessed his undying love for me in two pages of notebook paper, front and back. He wrote just like he talked--a lot. After I'd read the letter I stuffed it down into the waistband of my pants. My eyes glazed over at the mere thought of Ronnie. He said he loved me and that I was pretty. No one had ever said they loved me before. I just couldn't get enough of his words. I studied myself in the mirror and pulled my long brown hair around my face like a curtain. I imagined him brushing it back away from my face, kissing my lips and running his fingers through my hair. I dreamed of walking down the aisle to greet him, my white gown flowing behind me, taking his outstretched hand into mine. It was all so delightful. Grandma would have a total fit and I'd for sure get my head knocked off if she ever found out I'd gotten a love letter from a boy. Every day we'd write to each other. That was better than any kind of face-to-face relationship for me. Each letter was filled with love, and I replayed the pages in my head. I read them over and over until the pages became worn and wrinkled. It was not an exaggeration to say that this summer was the best of my life. I wanted to share all my thoughts and dreams with him. I looked forward to reading his words and feeling the warm glow flare once more in my chest, but every time I came close to him I panicked. There were a hundred questions flying around in my head. Since he lived close by, it only took one day for me to get his letters. Then I'd write back, so every third day I'd get his letter. I'd stick it down in the waistband of my pants to read when I got home. As soon as I could, I'd go to the back room and lie down on the old trunk we had back there, and I'd open the letters. If I heard Grandma's footsteps on the linoleum floor I'd drop it between the trunk and the wall. I kept the letters stuck down behind that old black trunk, which held all the stuff Grandma never used. This went on all summer. Every third day I'd send Ronnie a letter, and I would get one from him.

Then one day I heard Ralph the grocery store owner say to Grandma, "I'll bring the mail today for you." This was the day I expected to get a letter from Ronnie. My heart hammered in my chest and I froze with panic. I was dead. She was going to find out. I slipped into the kitchen where Grandma was standing and looking out the window. "I want to go to the post office today," I said to Grandma.

"No, Ralph's going to bring it today." I felt my face droop and I wrung my hands as I went to the back room to wait for my punishment. The bad part was the way Ronnie wrote out his passion for me. I was just going to die from embarrassment, never mind the lickin' I'd get and the names she was going to call me. I remember when she beat poor Bitty nearly to death just for sitting on her eggs! Oh why did I ever start something like this? We lived right by the store. How I wished Grandma would send me there for something before Ralph went for the mail so I could tell him to put the letter back for me, but that would be embarrassing to me, too. Besides, his helper was a little slow, and would probably blabber to Grandma. He was always knocking on the door, campaigning for High Sheriff. I wouldn't put it past him to bring the letter over and hand it to Grandma if he found it. I lay on the long trunk where I tucked Ronnie's letters and my *True Story* magazines down between it and the wall and fought to keep the lump from gathering in my throat. It took Ralph a couple of hours to decide to go to the post office. I got up and looked out the window. Ralph's car was gone. Fresh panic overwhelmed me and I didn't trust my legs for support. I sat on the old trunk waiting, my face burning. My anxiety continued to mount. Finally he came to the door and knocked. I straightened my spine and raced to answer it. Maybe I could find the letter and hide it before Grandma came out of the kitchen. He handed me the few envelopes but Grandma was right behind me. "Give me those," she said. I handed the batch to her, held my breath, and ran back into the back room, waiting for the shoe to drop. I watched out the window as Ralph and his helper sauntered back and disappeared through the door of the store. I waited a good while. No explosion.

What was she waiting for? Was she reading his letter? Studying every word? I wanted to get it over with. I had cupped my hands over my ears to muffle the sound of her outrage, but the house stayed quiet. Then I couldn't stand it any longer. I went back into the living room where she was slumped on the couch, looking through her mail. "What did you get today?" My voice trembled, and I swallowed hard.

"Nothing worth anything, just bills I can't pay. I guess we'll just end up in the poorhouse." Her voice was like a frayed thread almost worn through. We were always going to the poorhouse, to hear her tell it. I didn't even know what the poorhouse was or where it was, but any day we were going. She looked worried and laid the mail over to the side on the couch, then got up and walked through the house to the other room. Frantically I picked up the mail and sorted through it. Where was that letter? I looked down in the cushions, and under the couch, all over. There was no letter from Ronnie. I held my breath and let it go in a rush of relief, but in a way, I felt sad. Even though I would have gotten into big trouble with Grandma, I still enjoyed his letters. They came sporadically the rest of the summer, then stopped.

The next year, we were in high school. I passed Ronnie on the sidewalk and asked him how he was, and did he want to eat lunch together.

He looked me in the eye. "You think you can just treat me any old way and I'll come running back to you?" Then he turned and walked on. I looked after him for a few moments. My shoulders slumped, I blinked back tears, and my heart suddenly felt heavy, as I walked on to my next class. We never spoke much after that.

Jenny Sturgill

Pants

I rubbed the sleep out of my eyes, threw the covers off, and swung my legs off the my broken-down couch. Today was the first day of my sophomore year in high school, the day I had dreaded all summer. I sat and stared at Grandma's back as she stood by the window in the kitchen. I could tell her, but there was no use, she'd just fly into one of her raging fits and I wasn't up to it, especially today. Besides, she never would understand. She wasn't really there, she lived in her own world, and that world didn't include me. I got up and pawed through my clothes that hung on a wire stretched across the back wall. I picked out my faded black elastic pants and a loose white blouse. I decided the clothes were adequate enough to avoid any inspection or even notice. I slipped off my pajamas and eased into my drab outfit. Maybe old Mrs. Hanks, the English teacher I'd have this year, wouldn't see me.

I didn't realize then how much today would impact my life.

When I reached the grimy brick building that was Betsy Layne High School, I cut through the shoulder-to-shoulder crowd, squeezing my books so hard that the sharp edges cut into my arms. Waving to the friends I hadn't seen all summer, I hurried up the stairs to the classroom on the right. Maybe she wasn't here yet. I peeped inside. Good, her back was turned. She was busy writing something on the blackboard. I tiptoed to the back row and took a seat in the corner. She turned around, took more chalk from her desk drawer, and stuffed it into the pocket of her plain print dress that came down just to tops of rolled down white socks. She had thick black Groucho Marks eyebrows that were so prominent they made the rest of her face disappear. I hunched down in my seat. I was dead if she saw me. Stray locks of gray-black hair escaped a wadded bun on the crown of her head. She attempted to sweep the strands back away from her face with her chalky fingers. Her eyes flickered in my direction, and my heart skipped a beat, but she turned and studied the board, then continued writing. If you were caught passing a note, shooting a paper wad, or just looking like you might want to, she'd twist your ear so hard it turned beet red. Everyone was scared to death of her. Students snickered and whispered behind her back about how she let you grade your own test papers.

    I bowed my head and pretended to be

engrossed in my notebook. Soon the bell sounded and the class filled up. Mrs. Hanks turned to greet us.

"Good morning class," she said, then she leaned to one side and looked straight at me. My heart fluttered like a trapped bird.

"You back there in the corner with that white top on, stand up," she said. I eased out of my chair, straightened my blouse and managed to raise my chin for the blow. Mrs. Hanks' eyes pierced a hole clear through me until I thought I'd melt into a puddle and die. Are you wearing pants?" Those brows migrated together to form one black streak above her eyes.

"Yes ma'am, I..."

"Come up here at once." I walked toward the front. There sat that Andrea Williams, all full of herself, in the front row with her fresh pink dress bulging into the aisle. It had at least twelve petticoats under it, and she was swinging her leg like she had been crowned queen of the universe. I brushed past her and caught a whiff of strawberry bubblegum. Mrs. Hanks didn't allow gum in her class either. She was in for a big surprise. For an instant our eyes met. I forced a smile, managed to keep my head held high and kept going. I felt scorching eyes burning into my back.

Mrs. Hanks' eyes traveled slowly from my head to my toes and back to my hot face. Her overgrown eyebrows twitched. "You're excused from my class until you can wear decent clothing. I do not allow those vulgar pants in my classroom." I could feel the jagged corners of her words stabbing at my flesh. I felt naked as I turned and walked out the door.

"You can come back when you can abide by my rules," she called after me. "Miss Williams, are you chewing gum?" I heard her flinty voice say as I stepped out of sight. In spite of my anguish I just had to smile.

The other girls wore skirts over their pants, with the legs rolled up underneath. After class, they removed their skirts and rolled their pant legs back down. I didn't have a skirt, and was too embarrassed to ask my friends to loan me one. I raced down three flights of stairs as fast as I could to the restroom in the basement, out of sight. Thank goodness there was no one around. I felt like crying, but I didn't. I was used to being embarrassed by the things my grandma did and made me do. Like the way she emptied the chamber pot onto cars that parked in front of our house.

I suppose, in her eccentric way at some point

she had forgotten that I was a girl. I looked in the mirror and winced at my hair that Grandma had cut just the night before. It hung jagged and limp down the sides of my flaming face. I splashed cold water on my cheeks to help force the redness away, then I headed back up to the third floor study hall where I spent the rest of that hour.

The next morning I stopped by Mrs. Johnson's English class to see if she had an opening, but she smiled and said, "I'm sorry but my class is full, couldn't fit another soul in here." So I went back to study hall where I spent the rest of the year during first period.

When it came time to graduate two years later, I fell short because of that English course. I didn't know what to do. I didn't tell Grandma about the incident because she'd say it was my fault, that I was lying about the teacher and the whole thing. So I kept quiet.

The day before graduation I rapped lightly on the principal's door and inhaled a deep breath of courage, half-hoping he wouldn't answer.

"Come in," he yelled, with that deep voice of his. I eased inside and closed the door.

"What can I do for you, Jenny?" he asked. He knew my name and the names of all the kids in school, their sisters, brothers, moms, dads, uncles, aunts, cousins, dogs and cats. He stood up like a gentleman, his belly protruding over his belt buckle, and smiled a broad smile that lit up his whole face. He sat back down, removed his glasses, and laid them down on papers piled in front of him, then leaned back in his chair. We exchanged polite greetings.

I swallowed hard and spoke. "I have a proposal for you, Mr. Hanks." I managed to keep my quivering voice steady. He crossed his hands across the chest of his white shirt and smiled.

"Oh, and what might that be?" he asked. I told him about the day back in my sophomore year, about my grandma always making me wear pants, and that I had no explanation for that peculiar behavior of hers. I tried hard not say anything condemning against Mrs. Hanks. After all she was his wife. Everyone said he was just as scared of her as we were. I knew it was a long shot but I had to do something.

"Mr. Hanks... I'd," I swallowed, "I'd like to write an essay for you on how important it is to stay in school in exchange for my English credit." There, it was out. I held my breath and waited. Mr. Hanks rubbed his chin and stared at me, our eyes locked in silence, for what seemed like an eternity. I sat with my hands in my lap squeezed so tightly together that my knuckles hurt.

He leaned forward, picked up his glasses, put them on and studied me some more. "I suppose I could do that. Have it to me as soon as possible, but tomorrow night when you walk across the stage you'll only receive a blank piece of paper." His words tore through me like a knife. I thanked him kindly, shook his hand, and stepped out the door.

I never told Grandma about any of it and I don't know if Mr. Hanks ever read the essay or not, or if he just fudged the credit. I received my diploma two weeks later.

I got caught up on my English skills and finally figured out where to place my commas and semicolons. As for pants, I still wear them every chance I get.

The Hammer

I came home from school that day, pulled the door open and peered into the dimly lit house. I sniffed. The stench of soured whiskey and stale urine hit me in the face. It was an all-too-familiar smell. It meant that Grandma was on another drunken binge. I hated it when she was drunk. She got meaner, like the time I pin-curled my hair and got awakened in the middle of the night as she yanked the bobby pins out, hair and all. She got out among the neighbors when she was drunk, stirring up trouble with every one of them.

But today I got a cold, sinking feeling in my middle. The house was dark and quiet. My heart changed rhythm. Something was horribly wrong. I stepped through the door and eased it shut, then slipped past Grandma's room. The bed was made but the shades were drawn. That was strange; she always raised the shades during the day. I flipped on the light. Her grey bedroom slippers were still beside the bed. "Grandma, where are you?" My voice sounded weak, just barely a whisper. The living room was straight, the blankets for the sofa where I slept were folded in a neat pile on the floor, but the kitchen was a mess, pots still on the stove with dried oatmeal curled and stuck to the sides. Dirty dishes cluttered the table. Then I heard a moan coming from the extra bedroom in the back. I stiffened. No one ever slept in that bed, not since my cousin Edward had gone off to join the Marines. I should have gotten that bed when he left, but by then it didn't really matter to me. I was used to the couch. I heard another moan -- a sound like a hurt cat. I tiptoed to the door. I could barely make out a lump in the bed from the dim light that filtered under the window shade. I eased my hand along the wall and light flared. I blinked. Grandma lay in a bundle of twisted blankets. The smell of stale whiskey was stronger than ever. "My leg hurts," she slurred. Her matted hair spilled out on the pillow. Her face was pale and pinched, and sweat beads glistened on her forehead. I edged closer to the bed and lifted the covers to reveal her swollen thigh. She let out another loud moan. My gaze lingered on the knot on the side of her leg. A peculiar bulge pressed against her skin. I put my hand on her thigh, and she let out a scream.

"What happened? I think your leg is broken." I pulled the covers back down over her.

She winced and rubbed her leg. "I was out fixing the fence so those nasty old ducks of yours wouldn't get out again and fell over it. Some men came--oh God my leg--off the hill and carried me inside."

I turned to leave the room. "I'll call an ambulance, you need to go to the hospital."

"Like hell. I'm not going to no shitty hospital." She raised herself up on one elbow, pulled the brown bottle of whisky from under her pillow. Her hands shook as she unscrewed the lid and took a long swallow. My throat tightened and I couldn't say a word. "You better not call anybody. I'm not going anywhere!" Her voice was shaky and loud and slurred.

I turned my back and went into the kitchen, where I sat at the table. I stared for a long time at the worn-smooth linoleum of the kitchen floor. There wasn't anyone to help. None of the neighbors were reliable enough to call; besides she had driven a wedge between herself and every one of them. She had a brother who lived several miles away. I'd call him first thing in the morning.

I took some corn from under the sink and went to feed the ducks and straighten the fence. I picked up the hammer she had left on the ground and took it inside.

As I entered the door Grandma yelled, "You

get in here right now!" I went to her bedside and laid the hammer down on the table next to her bed. "How about getting me another bottle from the refrigerator?"

"No!" I said. "You have to go to the hospital!" I winced at the smell rising from the soaked sheets. "You can't lay there in that filth. I'll get you a dry gown to put on." My voice came out frantic and uncertain. Why did Grandma have to be so difficult? She'd rather lie in her own mess than to let me help her. It was as if I didn't exist where she was concerned, but she was like that with everyone. I couldn't even turn her over to get the dirty linen out from under her. But what would be the use, her mattress would be soaked through by now. I went into her bedroom, jerked open the dresser drawer and pawed around for something for her to put on. I found a pretty yellow gown that her daughter Jo had sent her. I slammed the drawer shut and stomped back into the bedroom where Grandma lay in the bed.

I slipped my hands around her shoulders and tried to pull her into a sitting position. "Oh God my leg, stop, stop, get out of here and leave me alone!" Her lips were set into a grim line, and she shoved me away. It was all I could do to keep my footing as she fell back against the bed. I turned and left the room.

The night dragged on. I went to bed on the couch in the living room. The only sound that came from the room was her moaning and the squeaking of the bed frame as she shifted during the night. I'd drift off from time to time only to be awakened by a scream from her. Finally I eased out of bed and slipped to the bedroom door. "Please let me call an ambulance," I said, as calmly as I could.

"Get out of here and leave me alone." Her eyes were small crescents and her voice shaky.

I went back to bed.

The next morning I stayed home from school. I found our old ragged address book and looked up her brother, Hobert. I dialed the number, hoping someone would answer. After four rings Hobert answered. Grandma and her brother weren't that close. He hadn't come around in years.

"Grandma's had an accident and I think her leg is broken," I explained. My voice quivered. "Can you come down here and make her go to the hospital?" My heart pounded harder and faster and I held my breath. Suppose he wouldn't come? Then what? I felt my knees go weak with relief, as he said that he'd come that afternoon.

I leaned against the doorway breathing the

stale air coming from the room. What if she died? Where could I go? I couldn't live here by myself. I couldn't live with my Aunt Jo, she had never asked. And besides, I wanted to graduate with my friends. I could go to live with Mrs. Akers, my fifth grade teacher. She'd once said I could, but that was a long time ago. I was in high school now, and I hadn't seen her in a long time. She might have changed her mind. I stayed in the kitchen and waited for Hobert. Finally I heard a car pull into the gravel driveway beside the house. I bolted out of my seat, and the scrape of the chair on the floor cut the silence. It wasn't Hobert but his daughter, Joyce, who got out and knocked on the door. She was short and stubby with eyes that didn't quite focus both at the same time, so you never knew if she was looking at you or not. Her face was flushed and she had a slow way about her. I hadn't seen her in a long time and remembered that she had always acted a little strange.

"Come in, I think Grandma has broken her leg. She's in the other room in the bed. Maybe you can talk her into going to the hospital." Joyce passed by me to the bedroom. I stayed in the other room, afraid my presence would just aggravate Grandma. Joyce came out and shook her head. "I didn't have any luck," she said. I felt panic rise up inside me. I didn't know what to do. Finally I called an ambulance despite Grandma's raging protests.

The ambulance screamed into to the driveway with its red lights flashing. Two guys wearing white coats came to the door. One was bald with a tiny black mustache above his upper lip. He wore a toboggan pulled down tight on his head. He had a quick smile that revealed perfect, straight teeth. The other one was tall and lanky with unruly black hair and long arms. He was wearing blue jeans under his white coat. I directed them to the back bedroom where Grandma lay.

They wheeled the stretcher into the room. "What happened here?" the bald one asked.

I explained about Grandma falling. "I think her leg is broken." I pulled down the covers and touched the knot on her thigh.

"Ma'am we've come to take you to the emergency room, you just need to sign this paper for us to take you." The bald man handed her a clipboard and a pen. He leaned over to place it in her hand.

"Get out of my house! I'm not going nowhere with you!" She snatched the hammer from under the covers and in a sweeping motion swung it at him. The man ducked and jumped back.

"I think we have a live one here," he said and chuckled. I couldn't help but remember the tale about Red Riding Hood and the big bad wolf. Grandma looked like the big bad wolf lying there in the bed. I rolled my eyes.

The tall guy turned to me. "We can't take her without her permission." I slumped back against the wall and sighed. They gathered their things and left.

I went back to the kitchen, and goose bumps rose on my arms as I stared into the emptiness.

I called her daughter, Jo, who lived in Atlanta, eight hours away. When she and her husband arrived I met them at the door with tender, drawn-out hugs. Jo was my favorite aunt, even though she'd never invited me to come live with her. It would have been no use, Grandma wouldn't even let me go stay with her for a visit. It made no sense; she wanted me there, but she always acted like she didn't, and threatened to send me and Edward to Pippa Passes when she got mad at us, whatever kind of place that was. She said Jo would just be filling my head with meanness. I wasn't allowed to write to any of my aunts and uncles and especially not to my mother. Grandma wouldn't even let me talk to her on the phone, and finally she quit calling. Jo came to visit more than any of the rest. She was fun and pretty and had blonde hair that cupped her heart-shaped chin. Her smile lit up her whole face. She was good to us and always remembered us at Christmas.

John, her husband, was a big guy with a potbelly and an easy way about him. His hair was combed back away from his face and you could still see the comb prints in it. Grandma liked him, and Jo was her favorite child. She often referred to her as "my baby." They went into the bedroom and I could hear yells and screams from Grandma as she told them to get out and leave her alone. They stayed a long time. She didn't like them *today*, that was for sure. I peeked around the corner and the stern expression on Grandma's face had gotten worse. I felt like I was in a nightmare, but my mind said otherwise. This was happening. They came out and told me they'd have to get a court order to have her admitted. Then they left. I wandered through the house, peeking in at Grandma from time to time to make sure she was still alive. What if they didn't get the court order? What would I do? Jo couldn't just leave me here all by myself, not with Grandma lying in the bed in a puddle of pee with a broken leg. She surely wouldn't do that, after all she was *her* mother. Grandma couldn't just lie there in that mess. I looked out the window every five minutes, twisting my hair into knots and holding back a scream. What was taking them so long? They said they'd be back...but would they? Tears burned my eyes. After hours dragged by they finally walked through the door. I wiped the wadded tissue across my face and sniffled. They looked more relaxed. "We got the court order. Jenny, call an ambulance." Jo went into the bedroom where Grandma was, and I could hear her voice softly telling Grandma she had to go to the hospital. I exhaled slowly as relief washed over me. Grandma was quiet.

The ambulance came and two different guys rolled a stretcher through the door. One was a thin man wearing glasses with thick lenses and shiny gold frames. The other one was short and had a pink roll of fat under his neck that wobbled when he spoke. We all went into the room. Grandma pulled out the hammer again but the one with the wobbly neck grabbed her wrist and took it away from her. She pounded their chests and tried to bite as they loaded her onto the stretcher, all the while yelling obscenities.

"I'll have you *all* locked up. You're nothing but a bunch of reprobates and sons-of-bitches! Get out of my house!" She swung her fist at the attendant. He dodged out of her way. Everyone laughed, which made Grandma even madder. "Glad you all are having yourself a good ole hootin' nanny at my expense! I'll show you!" She smirked. "You're all going to jail over this, you just wait and see." By now all the neighbors had come out to watch. She really did look like the big bad wolf. I chuckled silently.

We followed behind in Jo's car. I could hear Grandma moaning and screaming in my head even though I couldn't possibly hear her, that far away from the ambulance. We arrived at the emergency room. She continued to flail and scream as they rolled her into the hospital, swinging her fists at anyone who came near.

After she was settled in her room, Jo, John, and I went to Jerry's to eat. Any other time I'd have been thrilled to dine out in a real, sit-down restaurant, but I just stared at the menu. It was strange. I kept hearing Grandma hollering and moaning. I looked around the restaurant. It was as if she were over in a corner somewhere. My food came, but I hardly ate a bite. It was scary, like I was in another world.

I stayed at the hospital and slept wherever I could. Sometimes I'd sleep in an old wooden wheelchair I'd found in a corner of the hallway. In the middle of the night one night, two male aides

Jenny Sturgill

came, shook me awake, and made me get up. I wandered the hallways the rest of the night because there was nowhere else to sleep. She moaned and yelled all during the night, disturbing all the other patients. You could hear her all the way down the hallway, day or night. It was the first sound you heard when you stepped off the elevator. They ended up tying her to the bed so she wouldn't to get up and fall again. Sometimes the nurses would come in and give her a shot and she'd claw at them. They'd come out with welts on their arms where her nails had scratched them. Usually it required two nurses to handle her. I sat cross-legged on the slim cot they finally brought me to sleep on. My temples tightened and I pressed my forehead into my hands as she fought with the nurses. My face burned with embarrassment, and I wanted to just sink into the floor and disappear. She never ceased to amaze me with her meanness. The nurses spoke reasonably, in comforting tones, even. Most of the time they laughed at her and that made it not seem so bad to me, but when I was left alone with her all I wanted to do was drift into sleep and escape into the darkness. Jo hardly ever stayed at night. She would hand me a dollar for breakfast. In the mornings I sat in the cafeteria and ordered juice and two pieces of toast, revisiting the night, and hopeful that this journey was almost done.

One day, as Jo and I were walking down the hall I ran into Ronnie Allen from school and he asked if I'd quit. I told him no I had not. When we returned to Grandma's house later that evening, Jo said, "You told that boy you hadn't quit school. You have haven't you?" She sat down at the kitchen table. I jumped up from my chair, startled that she would suggest such a thing.

"No, no I haven't, I'm going back." I held on to the table with both hands.

"I can't stay here with Mother, I have a house in Atlanta. I need to get back." Her voice was loud and defensive. She squinted up at me in a calculating way.

"We could get someone to stay with her. I can't quit school, not now, not when I'm almost finished." My throat tightened and made my voice came out squeaky. A new fear settled on my mind. It could take months for Grandma to recover. Besides, that was the last thing I wanted to do with my life. I couldn't believe she expected me to stay home and quit school.

"But you've missed so much already."

"I can catch up, I can... I know I can! I can't

quit!" A wave of nausea came and went.

"We'll talk about it later. Right now, I have too much to handle without you starting something else." She slowly stood and left the room.

A few days later Grandma went to surgery to have a rod placed inside her broken femur. Jo was there with me. Edward was overseas. When they got ready to wheel Grandma away Jo said, "Hold her hand. Let her know you're here." A shiver ran through me. I shook my head no. I couldn't. I never remembered us ever touching in an affectionate way.

She was sick for a long time and stayed in the hospital for about a month. Grandma didn't want me out of her sight so I ended up missing a whole month of school. After staying at the hospital almost every night, I finally got to go home. After nights spent in straight-backed chairs and on that tiny cot, I was weary and could hardly keep my eyes open long enough to get to my couch. I fell asleep immediately and slept until way late in the morning when Jo nudged me awake.

Jo stayed for quite some time. I returned to school, studied hard, and got caught up with my schoolwork.

The Witch

My Aunt Jo sat on the bench in front of the dresser. "Are you about ready?" I asked, standing in the doorway of the bedroom. I shifted from one foot to the other and folded my arms across my chest. It was Saturday and I'd been looking forward to this day for a long time.

"Not yet." She raked the brush through her pageboy-styled blonde hair, turned and looked at me. "Besides, I have to fix Mother some lunch before we go." I went into the living room and sat on the couch to wait. I tapped my foot on the linoleum floor and squirmed in my seat. I couldn't wait to go see the witch lady. I'd heard about her all my seventeen years and felt a little kin to the witch population, since I had been born in a witch's house just up the road from where we lived. I had never met a witch, and I was excited and just a fraction scared, too.

"Hurry up and let's go." I followed behind her every step as she busied herself in the kitchen, fixing lunch for Grandma, who was in her bedroom in bed, still getting over her broken leg.

"We just might run out of daylight." She looked at me over her shoulder as she carried in a tray and placed it on the bed across Grandma's lap. Grandma inspected the food and scooted up in bed. Grandma was nice to Jo. She seemed to be the only one who didn't come under her wrath. Grandma always said that Jo could squeeze out tears at the drop of a hat. They sure seemed to work on Grandma. They never worked for me! Grandma finished her lunch of broiled chicken and carrots and we gathered the dishes and piled them up in the sink to wash later.

  I took down the tangerine jacket Aunt Jo had given me from the nail by the door and slipped it on. Aunt Jo got her yellow slicker from the bedroom and draped it over her arm. It was a gray, damp day, with drizzles of rain that made the roads slick. We piled into the car. The engine roared and we headed down the road and across the bridge to the edge of the mountain. Jo pulled the car over to the side of the gravel road, where the path went up the hill, the drizzle making it slippery.

  We followed the path upward. Sickly green weeds crept over the trail. Nothing moved in the landscape except the crunching of fragile branches under our feet and the scurrying of a rabbit among the leaves. Tall trees draped a canopy over us and the sky was dark. My stomach knotted as we climbed farther and farther up the mountainside. Jo spotted it first. The small two-story house just up ahead of us brooded under gnarled tree branches that curled like fingers. Moss the color of pond slime covered the roof. The porch sagged, and seemed to groan under its own weight. It was held up by small tree trunks. We edged closer. I could hear a low moaning sound, perhaps nothing more than the wind blowing off the top of the lopsided chimney. A breeze made the shutters tap against the house and the hinges squeaked. The house itself was a dark, sinister color and it didn't help that it was such a dark day. The steps up to the porch were old and worn. Cobwebs draped everywhere made me sick with fear, and the door knob sagged in a twisted fashion. There was no window in the door, only an eye hole. The windows were black, and panes were missing. They were patched with plastic that flapped in the wind, attached haphazardly to keep out the cold. The floor boards squeaked under our feet as we stepped onto the bare wood. I felt an unsettling feeling in my gut as we walked across the porch.

Jo raised her hand to knock, then her arm froze in mid air and she looked at me. "Are you sure you want to do this?"

Even though my stomach was tight I nodded

yes. She knocked on the door. We heard footsteps and a shadow fell across the sliver of light under the door. It creaked open and a woman stood in the doorway. She wore a dark colored dress that came just to her ankles, her dark hair was long and piled on top of her head. Strands had escaped and floated down to her shoulders. "What can I do for you girls today?" She smiled, revealing open spaces where her front teeth were missing. It gave her a vampirish look. She reached a bony hand toward us.

We hear you tell fortunes," Jo said. The woman took Jo's hand and pulled her inside. I followed behind and stood beside her, held my breath, and looked around. The room smelled of burnt wood and incense and was littered with old stacks of magazines and newspapers. A pile of firewood was stacked near the stove and there was a broken banister on the stairway that led upstairs. A bare wooden table stood in the small kitchen, surrounded by four straight-backed chairs. The iron wood-burning stove held a black cooker and a coffee pot, and a sharp ax stood by the door.

"I do indeed, honeys, come right over here, and have a seat at the table." She took my elbow and swept me along to a chair.

"Have a seat, I'll make some coffee, and we'll

see what your future holds. It only takes a minute for the coffee to brew." She went over to the stove, got the coffee pot, carried it over to a pail and dipper, and filled it with water. "Tell me a little about yourselves. Are you all from around these parts?"

My gaze fell on the ax leaning against the door. What if she killed us? Nobody would ever find us here. We shouldn't have come. We needed to just get out of here. I felt a cold chill that made my blood run icy through my veins and I forced myself to take deep calming breaths.

"I'm here from Atlanta taking care of my mother. She fell and broke her leg. This is my niece, Jenny." She looked at me and smiled. "She's been wanting to come see you ever since I've been here. My husband, John, stayed with Mother so we could come."

"Do you live here by yourself?" I folded my trembling hands on the table in front of me and looked the woman in the eye. She had dark sinister eyes that stared into mine. Would she grab the ax and whack off our heads? Suppose she was one of those people that killed you and then ate the body, and no one was ever the wiser? No one knew where we were, alone up on this desolate mountain with a witch woman.

"No, honey, I live with my husband. He's my second husband. He's out hunting, but he'll be back soon. My first husband died suddenly. He just died, we never knew what happened." She shrugged her shoulders. "Died right there in that chair you're sitting in." She pointed to my chair. I squirmed in my seat and looked down at the chair. "Sudden-like. After supper he just fell over dead." She bowed her head and stared at the peeling red polish on her long fingernails.

Sure, I bet she poisoned him. We should just get out of here right now, while the getting was good. Why'd we ever come here? I looked at Jo, but she seemed to be enjoying chatting with this murderer. She beamed and smiled and seemed relaxed. My heart speeded up.

Just then the door creaked open and I felt a rush of wind against my back. I looked around. In walked her husband, who was wearing a faded pair of overalls, muddy boots up to his knees, his dark matted hair sticking out around the edge of his worn hat, and eyebrows that were bushy and hung down over his eyes. He had a squared-off chin, and peg-like teeth that were too big for his face. He looked dangerous and mysterious. At his side hung a coiled rope, and he had a shotgun tucked under his arm. He lowered the shotgun and leaned it by the door next to the ax. I could smell the cold fresh air from outside. He closed the door and sauntered over to the table.

"Gettin' your fortunes read, uh?" He put his arm around the witch lady and gave her a squeeze. "She's the best, 'round these parts."

"Oh, go on with yourself, " she said, and smiled a bashful smile. "I think the coffee is just about ready." He sauntered off up the stairs. I could hear his footsteps and rustling sounds over our heads. Was he up there preparing our death trap? Was he going to hang us with that rope? I wanted to get up and run out the door, but I sat still as a mouse trapped in a corner.

The witch woman got up, went to the cupboard, and took down two cups and saucers. I watched closely to see if she was going to slip in any poison. She poured the steaming coffee into one, then the other and placed them both on the table before us. The steam rose up and warmed my face. I stared down at the liquid as black as the witch's eyes and said, "I think I've changed my mind, I don't like coffee and it was a mistake to come here." I looked over at Jo. "I think we better go." I started to get up and Jo grabbed my arm and pulled me back down. I felt a panicked lump rise in my throat.

"Why, honey? It's just one cup. I'll put in some sugar and milk, and that'll make it taste better," the witch lady said, with the corners of her mouth turned down.

"Well, I'm having mine done. You mean after all that begging to come here, you're not going to have yours read?" Jo's voice had gotten loud with irritation. I folded my hands in my lap and stared at the cup. "Please, let's just go."

"No, we're staying!" Jo lifted the cup, blew across the coffee, then took a long sip. She set the cup back down and it clinked against the saucer. I waited for her to fall to the floor. I looked at her, fearing the worst, but she just kept on sipping and chatting. Maybe the poison didn't work right away, but then there was that ax by the door. After Jo had drunk all her coffee, the witch lady took her cup, swirled it round and round, and stared at the grounds, then began to speak. She told Jo that she saw children in her future. Aunt Jo was approaching forty and had had several miscarriages. The witch woman went on and on about the wonderful life Jo was going to have. Jo let out a yelp and a smile stretched across her whole face. She grabbed my sleeve and shook my arm so much it hurt.

"See, go on, have yours read. The coffee isn't

bad, go ahead and drink it, she can put in some sugar to make it taste better." I picked up the cup and my trembling hand made ripples across the black liquid. I hesitated then said, "No, I don't want anything in my coffee." I lifted the cup to my lips and sipped the coffee. It tasted bitter. Grandma drank coffee. It smelled good, but I had never tasted it.

Finally I finished. Again she took the cup and swirled it around, leaving the grounds scattered around the bottom. She bowed her head and stared at the cup, making a groaning sound deep in her throat. My heart skipped a beat. Then she spoke.

"I see here you've had a hard time of it, dearie, but things are going to change. I see someone tall and lanky in your future. How old are you? She raised her head and looked me in the eye.

"I'm seventeen." I leaned in.

"He's very close to coming. He's in your very near future. You are going to have a long, happy, productive life. I see many children running around in your house."

"How many?" I leaned in closer.

"Several, like seven or eight." She bowed her head again. "You're still going to go through some hardships, but those things won't last long, you are headed for a good life."

Jenny Sturgill

Seven or eight children? I didn't even know if I liked kids or not. I hadn't even seen a newborn baby before. I liked the part about the tall lanky boy. I racked my brain, trying to think who that might be. There was Benson, who was a little sweet on me, but he wasn't by any means tall and lanky. Maybe it was Eugene, but he'd stood me up when I'd begged Aunt Jo to let me go out with him while Grandma was in the hospital. I went and waited at the door of the hospital where we were supposed to meet, but he never showed up. I can't blame him. I guess I stood him up first, when he ask me to the prom and Grandma said no. I told his friend Donald Ray to tell him I couldn't go, but he showed up all decked out in a suit, looking for me. He didn't believe me when I told him. I guess it was payback for me. I sighed. But he was tall but not lanky. Lanky means skinny.

The witch woman raised her head and smiled, I could see her pink gums where her teeth were missing in the front. A good life uh? I couldn't wait. I still wasn't convinced she wasn't going to kill us. New fear clamped the pit of my stomach. We all rose from the table. Jo dug inside her purse and pulled out some bills and handed them to her. The witch woman wadded the cash and stuck it deep into her dress pocket. I heard footsteps upstairs and her husband came down the steps. He walked over and picked up the ax and inhaled slowly, through wide nostrils. He grinned, and my heart stopped.

"I think I'll go out and chop some wood before it gets too dark."

We went quickly down off the mountain, arms wrapped across our chests against the chill. I was thrilled with my prediction and Jo grinned from ear to ear.

Jo seemed to believe all of the witch woman's predictions. I kind of doubted what the woman had said. Well, I doubted until that tall lanky guy came into my life and ended up becoming my husband. As it turned out he was someone whom I had seen around and had known all my life. And sure enough, my aunt Jo went on to carry a baby to full term and delivered a beautiful little boy. As for all the children running around my house, after having two babies within a year and three days I put a stop to that and prevented *that* prediction from coming true.

Jenny Sturgill

The Suit

As the sun broke through the window I yawned and stretched-full length. Maybe I could get dressed before Grandma woke up. She was still in bed in the other room. I tiptoed past Grandma's door to the back bedroom and took down my new--well, new to me--skirt and jacket from the wall. I pulled the oversized shirt over my head then slipped off my pants, stepped into the skirt, pulled it up over my hips, and slid into the jacket. My Aunt Jo had sent it to me after she had gotten tired of it. It was tweed, brown and yellow mixed. The skirt was fitted and the jacket was short and fit me well. Carrying my shoes, I tiptoed into the kitchen to get a bite of breakfast without waking Grandma. I opened the refrigerator, took out the milk and eased it onto the table. I poured my cereal and milk into a bowl and wolfed it down fast. If I was careful, I could slip out without having to deal with Grandma this morning. The school bus trundled past the window. When it went down the road I had about three minutes to get my books and be at the side of the road, ready to board it when it came back up.

Grandma hardly got out of bed anymore since she'd broken her leg. She could walk with a walker but seldom did. At least she didn't follow me around, yelling in my ear. She just beat on her mattress with a long stick she kept near her when she needed something, and yelled from her bed like a wild Comanche gone on the warpath, like the ones I'd seen in old western movies. She sure had a mouth on her. I'm sure the neighbors heard her bellowing all the time. I guess they got used to it. Sometimes when she was asleep, I'd sneak into the bathroom and wash my hair, but not very often. She still kept close tabs on me from her queen-sized bed. For some odd reason she still wouldn't let me wash my hair. I was lucky because it always looked the same. Not dirty and not clean. Once my friend, Patricia Roberts, from school, asked me why my hair never looked either clean or dirty. I shrugged and said I didn't know. I didn't want to tell her I wasn't allowed to wash my hair.

    We'd moved from our little four-room house where I'd spent most of my childhood into this house when I was a sophomore in high school. It had a real bathroom with a commode, a sink, and a tub. This one had five rooms. We still used the back room for junk and that's where I hung out most of the time. I felt like we were really coming up in the world. No more peeing in a lard bucket and emptying it into the one-holed outhouse, although I was surprised that

Grandma allowed Edward and me to use the commode. She had her eccentric ways of thinking. She still wouldn't let us use the tub. The first time I bathed in the tub was when she was in the hospital, and it was wonderful. My Aunt Jo had left some bubble-bath on a shelf in the bathroom. I poured in a little and turned on the faucet. The smell of honeysuckles filled the room. I tested the water on my wrist, undressed, and stepped into the tub. I eased myself down into the water and the bubbles surrounded me. I scooped some into my palm and touched them to my cheeks. They burst against my skin and I couldn't help but giggle. I gently blew them off my hands back into the water. The hot water swirled around my body. It felt delicious. I sank down into the tub and felt the most comfortable and warm sensation throughout my whole body. I could have stayed there forever. Grandma would be mad if she knew I was taking a bath, but she clearly didn't know what she was missing. I giggled out loud. It sure beat washing off with a rag in a pan of soap and water. I stepped out and looked down at the pink glow of my body. I couldn't wait for the next opportunity, but so far I hadn't gotten a chance. She still said that a bath was too big of a mess for her to clean up, although I had been cleaning up after myself for a long time now.

I was jolted back to reality by a blood-curdling yell from the other room. I grabbed my books from the table, and took one last look in the mirror on the living room wall. A young woman stared back at me. I tucked my hair behind my ears and then pulled it back out again. I turned sideways. I tugged at the skirt that came down below my knees. The jacket hit me just at the waist. I loved this suit and couldn't wait to see what my friends said about it. I smiled and hurried to Grandma's door to tell her I was leaving. She sat straight up in bed, looking like the Wicked Witch of The West. She just needed to straddle that stick and fly around the house. Her mouth hung open, her forehead crinkled, and her lips thinned. "Where do you think you're going with that on?" She swung her legs off the bed and grabbed her walker, gripping the handles so hard her knuckles went white.

"It's time to go to school." I know I sounded annoyed. I just wasn't up to a screaming match this morning.

"You're not wearing that, go get into something else right now." She stood and took a couple of steps, her walker making a thump on the bare wooden floor. I stepped back against the window and looked out. The bus was coming up the road.

"I don't have time to change. Besides, I don't

have anything else, all my clothes are ragged. I have to go. I see the bus." My head throbbed and my hands shook as I turned to go to the door.

"If that's the case then you're not going to school." Her face turned a blood red, her gaze as dark as the night as she looked me up and down. I felt small and naked. "You think you're something, all dolled up." Her tight smile turned her eyes into icy slits. I had remotely thought she might like the way I looked.

I always worked hard, trying to obtain just a grain of approval from her, but she never showed any signs of it. Good grades, bad grades. Good behavior, bad behavior, it didn't seem to matter; her reaction was always the same. One good thing about it was that I always knew what to expect. There were no surprises. Well, sometimes she would be so ridiculous it *would* surprise me at how sickly odd she thought. She needed help, but I certainly didn't know how to help her. I did feel sorry for her sometimes, like the time she made us Kool-Aid and forgot to put the sugar in it. Edward said it was terrible and we should tell her. I didn't want to, because I knew it would hurt her feelings.

"I have to go to school today. I have a biology test." It seemed that every time I had a test I had to miss school for some lame excuse she came up with.

Against the Wind

Sometimes it wasn't a bad thing. I might get to ride the city bus into town to pick up something Grandma wanted. I enjoyed going to town and seeing the hustle-bustle of the city. Sometimes I'd have a little change I'd saved to buy a bottle of nail polish at the dime store. But today, I stepped to the door, my fingers tightened around the knob, and my blood boiled. I felt like I was watching myself from outside. All the bad memories came into focus, anger swelled in my chest, but hate, hate required energy, an energy I didn't have.

"You better not go out that door." She grabbed my shoulder. I jerked away, opened the door, and went out onto the porch. The bus stopped in front of the house and waited. Grandma came to the door and propped the screen open with her walker. I stepped down the three steps. "I hope you die before you get back here. You're not worth the salt that goes in your food!"

I froze. Her voice chilled my blood, and I felt as though my life had just run out. I didn't look back and pretended not to hear her. A lump gathered in my throat and choked off my breath as I climbed up onto the bus and forced a crooked smile for Mr. Evans, the bus driver. I didn't know many of the students on the bus so I took a seat by myself. I looked out the window and thought about what Grandma had said. She wished me dead. The words ground into my heart. I turned my face to the window and my whole body shook with silent sobs. I couldn't stop. I could feel the stares of everyone on the bus, and I heard whispers behind me. Someone handed me a tissue.

    I climbed off the bus at school and there stood Sharon and Janet waiting for me. Sharon let out a wolf whistle. "Hey, where'd you get that beautiful suit?" She grinned and Janet joined in to say something about how nice I looked today. Their eyes met mine and their smiles faded from their faces. My eyes felt swollen and my heart hurt. I walked on past them toward home-room. They ran close behind me, pulling on my sleeve. "What's the matter, Jenny?" they both asked with shock in their voices. They looked at each other, confused. I hardly heard them. I managed a smile, turned away, and said nothing.

    I couldn't go back home, I thought, not after that. I could go stay with Mrs. Akers. She had told me once that she'd like me to do that. I'd have a grand time there. She'd let me wash my hair, probably take a bath, and I know she liked it when I made good grades. Maybe I'd just get on the bus that went up her way, go up to her door and say, "Here I am, I've come to live with you." Wonder what she'd say? She might have changed her mind after all these years. Maybe she didn't want me any more. After all, I hadn't seen her in a long time.

The bell rang for first class, and I couldn't stop crying. Absently I went to my French class with Ms. Burke. I sat down and laid my head down on my desk. Ms. Burke looked around and asked, "What's the matter back there? I straightened up, and wiped my face on the wadded up tissue I held in my fist.

"Nothing." My whole face felt swollen. Good thing I didn't wear make-up or I'd really be a mess. When class was over I bolted to the door, afraid she'd ask me again. I went to biology class and took a chair close to the front. Mr. Crider was a no-nonsense kind of teacher, baldheaded and a little potbellied. He gathered the tests in his hand and walked up and down the aisles, passing them out. I opened the paper and knew the first question. I pushed my worry aside. I'd studied hard, so I knew most of the answers. That got my mind off what Grandma had said for a little while. I turned in my paper and walked back to my desk. Then it hit me again. I couldn't stop the tears. I had no intentions of going home. What would Grandma do? She'd call all my friends and maybe some teachers. I didn't know. She'd probably hobble around the house looking like some crazed lunatic, cussing and probably hitting the bottle. I'd end up having to go back anyway and she'd be worse than ever.

I stood by the steps and waited on the bus that went up to Harold, where Mrs. Akers lived. What if she wasn't home, then what? What if she said no? I waited until the bus was full, staying to the back of the line. I eased toward the bus's steps. "Going my way?" The driver smiled at me. I took a step forward then stopped and shook my head no. He closed the door and drove off. I walked over and stood in line for my bus.

I didn't know quite what yet, but I sensed something was different about me. After the tears I cried for my former life had dried up, I straightened my shoulders and took a deep breath. I was done trying to please her. My one goal now was to somehow escape.

I stepped off the bus, lifted my chin, and walked into the house. The minute I entered the door the sour smell of stale urine and liquor hit me in the face. I stiffened and walked to the back room. As I passed her room I stole a sideways glance into the room. Grandma was stretched out in twisted, dingy sheets in a sliver of sunlight that passed through the curtains. Any other day I would have cowered behind the couch. But today, I was going to make the best of her drunken state. Tonight, while she lay passed out in her bed, I was going to wash my hair and fix myself whatever I wanted to eat. My fear of her was gone. I took off my new suit and hung it on a nail on the back wall, slipped into my ragged pants and shirt that served as my pajamas, and walked out into the kitchen. I opened the cabinet door, took down the peanut butter and jelly and made a sandwich. I'd never had peanut butter and jelly until my Aunt Jo made me a sandwich one night, when Grandma was in the hospital. It was now my favorite food.

"Come in here, you little smartass," Grandma yelled from her bed. I was no longer desperate for her to understand me. I was rescuing myself as surely as if I'd bolted out the door. The curtain had come down on my childhood on this day. I went into the bathroom, gathered the shampoo and a towel, locked the door, and turned on the water. I could hear Grandma yelling and banging her stick against the mattress in the next room. I turned on the faucet, stuck my head underneath, and felt the warm water run over my head.

I felt a smile spread across my face.

Jenny Sturgill

Getting Married

I saw Willie at his mother's grocery store, the tall lanky boy with the dark curly hair that spilled down onto his forehead. He wore a blue Future Farmers jacket, faded blue jeans, and kept his hands thrust deep into his pockets. He was at least six foot two or three with shoulders and chest to match. I noticed his strong slim face with high cheek bones and narrow eyes and felt myself drawn to him. I felt an odd tingling beneath my skin. I don't think he even noticed me leaning against the counter, looking for my favorite candy bar. He was standing by the furnace grate in the floor. That's where everyone gathered to get warm. Some pulled up chairs and put their feet on it and when they did, the smell of burning rubber was heavy in the air. *What if I marry that boy?* I thought. I didn't think about it again after that.

A few months later, when I was eighteen, Edward brought him down to our house. They had both joined the Marines and were stationed together. We began talking and he asked me for a date. I looked up and our eyes met and held. I said yes. I always looked forward to his visits to see Edward. I liked him, he was fun to be around, came from a nice family, and we always had a lot to talk about. Why not go on a date? An excitement gathered in my stomach. I knew Grandma probably wouldn't let me go, but I really wanted to go. Grandma was drinking that day, but I just kept quiet instead of trying to get her to stop. It seemed that she never would get to the point of drunkenness. I hoped she'd just pass out and I would go while she slept it off.

My gray eyes sparkled and I couldn't help smiling at myself in the mirror. I'd never been to a drive-in movie before, or on any kind of date for that matter. My stomach was in knots, twisting, and churning as I got ready. I wished I had something pretty to wear. Instead, I donned my faded drawstring black pants and rose-colored shirt, pulled my hair back away from my face, and secured it at the crown with a pretty rhinestone barrette. Then I smeared on some rose pink lipstick. The whiskey had finally taken hold of Grandma, and she lay crumpled in a drunken heap among the dingy white sheets.

The sun had already begun to slide behind the horizon and the house was dimly lit when Willie came to pick me up. I climbed into the front seat and scooted as close to his side as I could. He reached down and took my hand, his grasp gentle but strong, his fingers curled around my palm. He was smiling from ear to ear. His touch was particularly enjoyable. A warm, happy feeling flowed over me, and a puff of cool air blew through the open window and stirred my hair. Goosebumps rose up and down my arms. We drove off up the highway toward the drive-in.

The movie was good, what I saw of it between long passionate kisses. When it was over, we came straight home. We pulled into the weed-choked driveway, and Willie put his arm around me and kissed my lips. His lips were warm and tender against mine, and a warm tingle flowed through me. I hated to leave his side and go in to face the wrath I knew would follow. If Grandma had sobered up she'd be chomping mad. I wanted to stay in the comfort and safety of his arms, but I sighed and let my arms fall from around his neck. "Thank you for such a good time." I climbed out of the car and leaned against the door.

"See you next week?" Willie called through the open window. I stepped up on the porch, paused, took a rippled breath, and glided inside, hoping Grandma would still be passed out. No luck. She had sobered up some. She sat straight up on the side of the bed.

"Where have you been?" Her words split my ears as I stood in the doorway of her bedroom. She pressed her lips together in a straight line, as she stared at me. "Who've you been running up and down the road, frigging with?" Her voice came out like a creak. The familiar slap of humiliation stung my face, and I felt my cheeks warm up. I resented every word that came out of her mouth. My nerves were unsettled by the time I got done listening to a raging recount of my shortcomings.

"Grandma, I haven't been frigging with anyone. We just went to the movies." I slid past the door to the living room. Grandma lay between the wadded up sheets, yelling at the top of her lungs until way into the night, offering up strangled accusations. She finally fell asleep. Spit had gathered along her lips and bubbled with each rise and fall of her chest. Her gray hair lay in a tangled mess on her pillow. I looked down at her and wondered what would ever become of her. She surely had a twisted mind. Normal everyday living was a struggle for her and for everyone around her. Like the time Edward's mom had come to help take care of her after she broke her leg. Grandma had run her off, saying she was hiding in the bathroom and taking drugs.

*

Willie and Edward would drive all the way from North Carolina to Kentucky on Friday night and head back every Sunday evening, getting there Monday morning, just in time to go to work. Willie and I saw each other on the weekend for the next week or two. We never went out on another date, we stayed there and talked at home. Grandma tolerated that as long as she could keep an eye on us. Then two or three weeks later, Willie called me from Camp Lejeune. "Will you marry me this weekend?" he asked. "We can go to Clintwood, Virginia, to do the job." Clintwood was a place where people could get married without any questions asked. It was a few hours east of where we lived in Kentucky.

Willie was a good boy. He joked a lot and his eyes twinkled when he teased, but he always made me laugh. He was honest, and if he promised to do something he would do it. If he said he'd be at Mr. Howard's to plow his garden he'd be there at eight A.M. sharp, as promised. He respected his elders, was good to his mother, and spoke kindly to Grandma, even though she cussed him a lot and talked hateful to him. I was stunned at his request. We had only known each other for a few weeks. My breath caught in my throat and I weighed the question. Could we really pull it off? "Yes, I'll marry you," I whispered.

"Just be ready and I'll pick you up at eleven o'clock." I hung up the phone and studied the proposition. I was in love, wasn't I? That's what you did when you were in love, got married. I didn't have money for college, so that was out of the question. I went about devising my plan to get away without letting Grandma find out what we'd planned. I sneaked into the closet and took down an orange flowered dress my aunt Jo had given me, and my dressy white graduation shoes, and stuffed them along with some other things into a suitcase that always sat under the window. After filling the suitcase with my clothes, I carefully placed it back exactly in the same spot in the back room where it always stood, so Grandma wouldn't know it had been packed.

She knew something was up, though. I could see it in her shifting eyes. "You're up to something, I can tell," she said as she limped through the door of the back room on her walker, her eyes wide and wild, looking at everything in the room. She went to the closet and pawed through my clothes, but decided all was well. I held my breath as she looked around. Her eyes fell on the suitcase standing under the window, but she seemed satisfied that it was as usual and didn't pursue it any further. She took one last look around the room, turned, and hobbled back to her bed, her walker thumping against the wood floor with her every step.

Willie had a friend, Mack Cecil, who was going to get married to his girlfriend the same weekend. It was to be a double wedding. Mine and Willie's and Mack and Mary Linda's. We would all ride in the same car. I couldn't wait, but I was scared, too. What would Grandma do when I walked out with that suitcase?

Saturday finally came. I parted the curtains and peered out the window every few minutes, watching for them to pull into the driveway. Finally I heard the roar of the motor and the crunch of the tires on the gravel. I ran to the back room, lifted the suitcase from its spot under the window, and carried it into Grandma's bedroom. Grandma was lying on the side of the bed. Her eyes grew big as she saw me with the suitcase in my hand. I swallowed hard and let out a deep breath. My throat felt tight. "I'm getting married today," I whispered. She'd always said she didn't care if I got married, I just wasn't going to date, which made no sense to me. How was that supposed to happen? Her brows rose and her mouth twisted into an ugly snarl.

"No you're not, not if I have anything to do with it." She scooted to a sitting position on the side of the bed, grabbed her walker, stood up, and hobbled to the doorway. I raced out the front door as fast as I could. Grandma followed me outside, yelling obscenities. "You think you're something with that suitcase hitting your hind end, running off here, leaving me by myself." Willie opened the trunk and I threw my suitcase in with the other luggage and closed the lid with a loud thump. He opened the rear door and I climbed onto the seat. Willie slid in beside me, gave me a quick peck on the cheek, and took my hand. We drove off. I turned to look back, and I could see her still standing on the porch, a wild look on her face, shaking her fist, and holding on to the walker with the other hand. She looked small and helpless. I felt a rush of guilt. What was I doing getting married? I was barely out of high school and I hardly knew Willie. This was crazy, but I didn't have too many options to choose from. I strained to collect my thoughts.

Soon my fears faded with the excitement of the day. My wedding day!

We stopped at Willie's mother's grocery store. Willie's sister, Barb, came out and stuck her head into the window of the car. "You better stop along the road and think about this for a long time," she chided. But we didn't listen, we just drove off up the road toward Virginia. I swayed back and forth in the back seat as the car went around one curve after another. The trees and mountains whizzed by the window in a fuzzy haze. My stomach rolled and churned, the blood drained from my face, and I tasted bile in the back of my throat. Finally, I could no longer keep control of my stomach. I ask Mack to pull over to the side of the road. Willie took my arm and helped me crawl out of the car. The air was damp and smelled of wet leaves. I bent over, wadded my hair behind my head, and upchucked beside the road. It splattered on the ground, barely missing my shoes. I crawled back in the car, opened my purse and took out a stick of cinnamon gum and popped it in my mouth to take the taste away. Willie put his arm around me and I laid my head on this shoulder. Could I really go through with this?

    My stomach had settled somewhat by the time we got into the town. We pulled in at a service station. I got out and opened the trunk, snapped the latches on the suitcase lid and took out my dress. It was an orange flowered pattern on a cream-colored background, made of some kind of chiffon material that felt good next to my skin. I picked up my shoes.

With my dress draped over my arm and my shoes in my hand I went inside and asked the attendant for the key to the restroom. I opened the door and stepped inside. The air was heavy with the scent of stale urine, and my stomach lurched. I felt as if I was going to upchuck again, but I managed to keep it down. Toilet tissue was strewn all over the floor and some stuck to the bottom of my shoes. The floor was shiny with what I imagined was urine, and the commode had a black ring around the inside of the bowl. I looked into the dingy mirror and a pale young girl looked back at me. I looked like I was about thirteen. I ran my fingers through my long brown hair and pulled it around my face and shoulders. I smiled and it came out crooked and fake. I felt hot so I splashed my face with cold water. What was I doing? I shook the thought from my mind and hurriedly changed into my dress and shoes.

  We arrived in town, drove down the street, and got our blood tests. Then we went back to the courthouse. We stepped through the door and joined other couples getting married that day. The room was long with low ceilings, a stuffy smell, worn hardwood floors, and was dimly lit by a single light overhead. Over in the corner, a middle-aged woman sat behind a cedar desk. A black-and-white photograph of a family stood at her elbow. The woman had a bit of restlessness in her smile. I quickly looked around and spotted the bathrooms down the hallway, just in case my stomach acted up again. I really didn't know what to expect. There was a whole line of couples giggling, talking, holding hands, and studying their feet as they waited. My excitement rose and I suddenly felt quite joyous, standing among them. We fell in line behind Mack and Mary Linda. The Justice of Peace was an old man named Otis Crabtree. He was pencil-thin and sat in a metal folding chair, dressed in a dark suit with a thin tie. He looked up at us from beneath big bushy eyebrows that were peppered with grey. He was a no-nonsense man whose presence matched his authority. From the back of the line I'd hear him say, as he married each couple, "Now I pronounce you husband and wife, next!" Then he'd wave that couple away and go on to the next one. When it came our turn we held hands and stood above him, anxiously waiting to say our vows and place our rings on each others' fingers. Before we knew what had happened he was waving us away. I hesitated for a moment until he shooed me to go on. I didn't even have time to think about what I was saying and what was taking place. The ceremony lasted only a few minutes or it might have even been seconds. It was very different from the way I had imagined it on my way there. We stepped away with our mouths hanging open. It reminded me of an assembly line. Disappointment welled up inside me. I felt as if I was floating, as if I wasn't even there, but I was. I could feel Willie's strong hand clutching mine. Wasn't this supposed to be special? It felt so mechanical, so ordinary. This was our special moment and it was over before I could even grasp the meaning of the words we had exchanged. What did it all mean? I forced a big smile, held my head high, the way I always did when I had no control over my circumstances, and shook the thoughts out of my mind. We were married and that was that. Hand in hand and we walked out into the bright sunlight. I didn't feel any different than I had when I went in. We settled into an awkward silence. Shouldn't I have been changed somehow? I was married now, really married. I didn't exactly know what that meant, but I was a married woman.

We didn't have much money to spend. We'd borrowed one hundred dollars from the bank to get rings. We found a cheap motel with a sputtering neon sign and got a room. Then we went to the grocery store for bread, bologna, a small jar of mayonnaise, and a couple bottles of soda. I was surprised at how hungry I was. We ate on a rickety picnic table outside the motel with Mack and Mary Linda. That was our wedding supper. I watched the frost form on the bottle of RC Cola as we exchanged smalltalk, and though the future was anything but certain, we planned it there on that table. We would get a place close to the base where Willie was stationed. I'd go with him as soon as arrangements were made. Grandma would have to stay by herself. She was capable. She could walk with her walker, and sometimes she'd be clear through the house before she realized she had walked off and left her walker in another room.

When it came time to go to bed, my hands trembled as I opened the suitcase and took out the ruby negligee Willie had bought me for our wedding night. I'd never had sex before and didn't know too much about what was going to take place, just what I'd heard from other girls and the guesses that Judy and I had come up with. The room was dimly lit, with only a bed, a night stand, and a worn flowered chair in the corner. I went into the small bathroom, locked the door, slipped off my clothes, and stepped into the negligee. It fit my ninety-six-pound body well. The top was snug around my breasts and the bottom was like a bikini with a short thin skirt that circled my hips. I unlocked the door and stepped out. "You look beautiful," Willie said and smiled. I could feel the blood rushing to my cheeks. We got under the covers and made love, then Willie fell asleep. He'd been up so long, driving from North Carolina all night. I didn't see what all the ruckus was about with Grandma and sex. Like it was some forbidden thing that by all means you should never do or even think about. She had made it out to be such a big deal, the one thing she tried to save me from.

I felt guilty and changed, somehow. I wanted to take a bath, but I didn't want Willie to see me naked, so I raised up and slipped the pillowcase from the pillow and wrapped it around me so he couldn't see in case he woke up. I fumbled around under the covers and found my negligee, eased out of bed, tiptoed to the bathroom door, and slid my hand around until I found the lightswitch. I squinted as the light flooded the room, then I locked the door and looked in the mirror. They said you looked different afterwards, and people could tell just by the way you looked. Did I look different? I turned my head from side to side, up and down, and peered into the mirror. I shrugged. I couldn't tell any difference. I turned on the faucet and filled the tub with the hottest water I could stand, eased myself down into the tub and leaned back. Right now, I could see the disgust that would be on Grandma's face when I got back. She'd know what I'd been doing. I could only imagine what she would say.

The next day we drove back to Willie's folks' home. It was Sunday and they had just returned from church. The whole family greeted us with well wishes and good cheer. Mrs. Sturgill had dinner cooked. "Fix yourself a plate and let's eat," she said to me.

"That's okay, I'm not hungry," I said, and took a seat over on the gold sofa pushed back against the wall. The tiny apartment was attached to their grocery store and there wasn't enough room for all of us to fit around the table. She fixed me a plate and brought it to me. Piles of fresh, hand-whipped mashed potatoes, slow-cooked chicken, green beans, and corn, all fresh from the garden, plus a big slice of cornbread. I'd never had anyone fix me a plate before. I took the plate and she smiled, gave me a tight hug, told me it would be okay, and I believed her. Everyone ate wherever they could find a seat. The chatter around the room was enchanting. I had never known such acceptance. This was a turning point in my life. I feel sure it was God's plan.

I had to go back home after Willie left to go back to base. Grandma had cooled off some. I stepped through the back door and set my suitcase down next to the couch, at my feet. She was sitting on the edge of the sofa and she glared at me. I sat down beside her and offered her a halfhearted smile. I uttered a meek "I'm sorry," but she did not respond. The house had settled into a wounded silence. Her face was pale and tinged with anger, her eyes lowered, her gaze fixed on some spot on the floor, her brows knitted into a frown. Her lips parted. She pushed fine gray hair back behind her ears, and took a deep breath. "What did you wear on your wedding night?" A note of accusation colored her voice. I looked at her, confused, and gave her a sideways glance from beneath my eyelashes. This was not the reaction I had expected. I knew she'd be angry, but she was somewhat subdued. She looked at me and her gaze traveled slowly up and down my body. My cheeks began to get hot, and I felt tired and unsettled. What a strange question, coming from her. I opened the suitcase, pulled out the crumpled red negligee Willie had bought me for our wedding night, and held it up for her to see. "You've fixed yourself now. You're probably pregnant." She said it like it was something nasty, almost whispering it. I pretended to be absorbed in the hem of my shirt and I rolled my eyes. I shuddered at the prospect, and could hear nothing but my own breath. My stomach felt tight, and I closed my eyes, trying to think clearly. Without another word she got up and went into the bedroom.

A few weeks later I went to live with my new husband in North Carolina. We got along well and got to know each other. We were so poor that we'd save up pop bottles to turn into the store for ten cents so that we'd have enough gas for Willie to get to the base and back. I spent my days sewing and cleaning the little camper in a trailer park that we lived in. I waxed the outside of the trailer with floor wax which turned the pink tin to a lighter shade of pink. It was so small that when you let out the sofa to make the bed you could put your foot in the bathroom on one side of the bed and put your other one into the kitchen. When the men had to leave to go somewhere overnight, I'd stay with Mary Linda. We'd cook, eat, and have a good time talking, way into the night. Mary Linda had gotten pregnant and was having morning sickness. We'd get up and make pancakes with flour and water. She'd eat them, go upchuck, then come back and eat some more.

Each payday we'd save up our quarters to buy a hamburger at the little stand down the road. But we were happy. We'd target shoot for recreation. Ammo was cheap and it was fun. We got married in September and, not knowing much about birth control, I became pregnant in February.

In the meantime, Willie was discharged from the service, and I went to stay with his folks. His mother was always laughing, and his father was the most humble man ever. They took me under their wing. Once my Grandma called and told me to do something. When I told Willie's mother, she shook her head and said, "No, you're mine now."

Erlan, Willie's mother, had a joyful way about her. She'd joke and double over laughing. There was something engaging about her laughing eyes. Her dark hair was smooth and shiny, swept back from her face and gathered in a roll around her head. Everyone liked her. Rufus, Willie's dad, was just plain sweet. He had a bowl of white hair and blue eyes that were alert and intelligent, a man who seemed to drift instead of walk. When he laughed it was soft. He was humble and spoke softly, in a slow southern drawl, a good Christian man, who always put the Lord first in his life.

Our first daughter was born in November of the next year, and I was alone and scared. Willie had gone to Michigan for work, and he couldn't be with me. Rufus had taken me to the hospital and dropped me off. I had about six hours of labor before I was put under ether to deliver. That evening I was lying in my bed, waiting to eat dinner. I hadn't seen Dawn yet. Willie's sister, Barb, who worked there in the hospital as an LPN, came to the door and asked, " Do you want to see her?" I said yes, but I really wanted to wait until dinner was over. I always like to save the best for last. She brought in this soft little bundle, wrapped in a cozy pink blanket. My gaze lingered on her tiny fingers, her sweet toes, and the wisps of dark hair that curled around the top of her head. When I took her, I felt an overflowing love. I sat completely still and looked down into her eyes. Such a warmth rushed over me that I forgot all else; it was just me and her, alone there in the cocoon of my blankets.

She was the first baby I had ever held in my arms.

We were living in Michigan when Gina was born the following year. It was a cold night, and Willie was at work when I went into labor. I felt a gush of water that ran down my legs and pooled on the floor. He didn't get off from work until midnight, and we left for the hospital as soon as he got home. The car door on the passenger's side wouldn't shut, so I rode all the way to the hospital clutching the door handle. Gina was born about two hours after we arrived. The nurse held her up so that I could see her, and her chin was trembling. She's cold, I thought. Then they laid her in the crook of my arm and I felt a surge of love rush through me at the sight of this precious bundle, so soft and innocent in my arms. I loved my children because they were mine, born of my body and entrusted to my heart. I wanted nothing but the best for them.

Jenny Sturgill

Epilogue

My life wasn't easy after I got married, but I was resolved to making a good life for our small family. We settled in Louisville, Kentucky. Willie found a good job, and we bought a house. Determined to put Grandma and her craziness behind me, I worked hard at developing a loving relationship with Willie and our two girls, Dawn and Gina. I always had a drive within me that had been fueled by encouragement from some good teachers. I learned about life and how to give of myself from a good counselor, and by paying close attention to other people's interactions with their children, family, and friends. It wasn't easy, but I learned to give them the love and understanding I never had. It took many years of trial and error, pure diligence, and patience. We are close now and have a good relationship. Every third Sunday we have the kids and the five grandchildren over for a night of pizza and a good time.

As for Grandma, she lived alone for awhile, then ended up in a nursing home. I went back to visit her when I could and found that she had mellowed out some. I never developed the relationship with her that I had tried so hard to achieve. I guess she was too angry at the world and her plight. The nursing staff at the home babied her some, and she seemed to enjoy the attention. She died of a massive stroke a few years after I got married.

After Edward finished his time in the Marine Corps, he married and had two fine boys. He found a job with an insurance agency. Having the gift of gab and an outgoing personality, he made a big success of his career, winning many awards for his excellent sales record. After he and his first wife divorced, he married a good Christian woman who led him to walk with Jesus. Later he opened up his own business and became very successful. We still see each other and are very close, even though he doesn't live nearby. We sometimes take vacations together. He's fun to be around and also seems to have gotten over his childhood with Grandma. He turned out to be a good Christian man, and a loving husband and father.

I taught myself to sew and spent the early years of our marriage making our clothes. I made Willie a leisure suit, and I made a sport coat for Willie's dad, which he wore proudly and often. Working at home when our children were small, I sewed for a fabric store, making their displays. I could choose any kind of fabric and pattern and make them any size. The store displayed the garments for six weeks and when it was time to take them down, they were mine, The clothes were my payment. I made all our clothes that way for many years.

When the girls were in high school, my dream of going to college came true. I had given up thinking about a career in writing, since it seemed hard to break into and the pay was poor, and so I decided to seek a degree in nursing. It was extremely hard, but I was determined to graduate with honors. I ended up graduating with a 4.0 grade point average. I was thrilled and to this day I'm proud of that accomplishment. It took a lot of long, hard work. In the evenings the girls and I would gather around the kitchen table, spread out our books, and study. I found it brought us closer together and sometimes I'd teach them something interesting that I was studying. The girl's grades soared to above average. After graduating from college, I took a job at a local hospital where I worked in many departments. I learned so much from the challenging workplace and having the huge responsibility for patients and their wellbeing. Then I took a job as case manager at the Norton Suburban Wound Treatment Center. I loved my work and put a hundred and ten percent into my career. I became certified in hyperbaric medicine and used my skills there to help people manage their non-healing wounds. In the meantime the girls got married and started having children. They both have good marriages, and they are good parents to their children. Together, Willie and I have raised good children who have become responsible, loving adults.

    Now that I've come into the autumn of my life I can look back on the years with a forgiving heart. I think of Grandma and all her crazy ways and realize that she probably did the best she knew how. She had no friends, was on her own with us to care for and only her children for what little support she had. She was a woman who had been dealt a sorry hand of cards. Her husband had gotten killed early in their marriage, leaving her to raise her five children alone, with no means of support. She was a proud woman who had to depend on welfare to make ends meet. And they didn't, most of the time. I can put myself in her place and wonder if I could have done it alone, as she did. How lonely she must have been. She was angry and resentful and maybe rightfully so. Life had been cruel to her. When Edward and I were born, our births sent another wave of anger and resentment boiling inside her. In that era, it was a disgrace to be born out of wedlock. I imagine how she must have felt, there in those little rundown rental houses, not knowing where our next meal was coming from. She didn't cry often. Once, when we had moved from a house we had lived in for many years, I found her was sitting on the side of the bed with her head in her hands, weeping. I can still see her, sitting there in her flowered house-dress, her gray hair falling around her hands as they covered her face, her shoulders shaking, and great racking sobs coming from behind those wrinkled hands. I stood in the doorway and watched, wanting desperately to go over and put my arms around her and comfort her. I wonder to this day how she would have responded. Would she have pushed me away or would it have comforted her? She had no one she could turn to for help. No one to give her advice, no one whose shoulder she could cry on. She probably loved us, even though she didn't show it. She had very few pleasures in life, just hard work and more hard work.

It was at Grandma's funeral that I saw my mother again. I was twenty-two, standing there beside my Grandma's casket, feeling sad for the relationship we never had, and feeling somewhat relieved that she was now out of my life. My mother walked up the aisle at the funeral home and I didn't even know who she was. I thought she was just another visitor. It had been eighteen years since I'd seen her. I greeted her politely as she approached. She had short, curly, bleached-blonde hair and she carried a few extra pounds. Her eyes were red, and she sniffled into a wadded tissue. To my surprise, she opened her arms and hugged me. I smelled liquor on her breath.

"Hello, Jenny, I'm your mother, Betty," she whispered in my ear. Resentment boiled up inside me and I pushed her away. I had waited patiently for many years for her to rescue me from Grandma's mean ways. All my years spent waiting for her to come back came rushing to the surface. I could think of nothing else. My legs were shaking, my throat tightened, and I couldn't speak for a moment.

"You never came back and you promised me you would!" The words finally burst out and I turned my back to her in anger, walked closer to the casket, and massaged my temples with my thumbs. I was conscious of her eyes on me, then she touched my arm. Her hands shook.

"Please listen. Charles wouldn't let me. He said we had too many bills to pay without another mouth to feed." Tears beaded her eyelashes, her face was pale, and her bloodshot gaze met mine. She and

Charles had a son, my half brother, Jack. She said they didn't have much money, and they had to pay for Jack's swimming lessons. This was a real punch in the gut. Swimming lessons? I had nothing to wear and she was paying for swimming lessons for her son? How fair was that? My heart felt heavy as I turned and walked away from her. Cold flowed into my body. She followed after me as I turned my back to her. We settled into an awkward silence. She was polite during the funeral. We spoke, but it was always guarded and strained.

After the funeral, she went on back to California. Letters started arriving from her, she wanted a relationship with me. She wanted me to call her Mother. I just couldn't. There was simply too much hurt. Then she developed breast cancer, had surgery for a mastectomy, and steadily went downhill. She died when she was in her forties, a short time later. I felt guilty, and I've regretted not developing that relationship with her. If I had, I wouldn't have all these unanswered questions about my father, whose blood runs through my veins. I've always wondered what happened between them, that they separated. Did he even know about me? What was his reason for abandoning us? Grandma said that he had sent my mother a bus ticket to come to him, wherever he was, and they had cashed it in to buy food.

I feel like I have a void in my life, without any details. After all these years, I realize how much I really missed out on. My mother had her reasons, more than a child could understand, but I could have worked through them as an adult and come to some kind of closure. Her letters and a cracked, faded picture of her are still in my memory box and I take them out from time to time and reread them. To this day I wish I had given her a chance. There are always two sides to every story, and I know that, for whatever reason my mother left me behind, she loved me.

In my later years, I've circled back to my dream of becoming a writer. I found a good writing school and rediscovered my love for writing. A whole lot of hard work has gone into my writing. After I finished the course, I saw several of my stories published. What a thrill that was, to see my name in print for the very first time.

I look back on my life with thanksgiving for all the opportunities God has given me. I'm still married to that tall, lanky boy that I first saw in the grocery store. Our marriage has stood the test of time. We've had a good life together, not because it was easy, but because we made a commitment and worked hard toward making it last. We had our differences, but they never got bigger than our love for each other. God blessed us with patience and understanding, and a willingness to hang on tightly to one another when the storms of life raged.

I've come to realize that it's not what a person does in life--incredible achievements, a fancy title, or a big paycheck. It's about putting yourself out there so that others can love you. I've learned that the thing that matters most is to be generous with yourself.

I don't know how far I've come, but I've learned that it's not what you have but what you share with others that matters. It's not where you started but where you end up that counts.

The End

ABOUT THE AUTHOR

Jenny Sturgill is a writer and an RN who lives in Louisville, Kentucky with her husband. She started writing after many years of nursing as a case manager for the Norton Suburban Wound Treatment Center. When she's not writing she enjoys gardening and cooking. She has written essays, short stories, and articles which were published in The Kentucky Explorer, Page&Spine Literary Magazine, Long Story Short, The Storyteller, Ky Story, The Enchanted File Cabinet, and The Pink Chameleon.

You can contact Jenny at jenny.sturgill@aol.com

www.ingramcontent.com/pod-product-compliance
Lightning Source LLC
Chambersburg PA
CBHW030323080526
44584CB00012B/689